Anonymus

Choice poems and lyrics

Anonymus

Choice poems and lyrics

ISBN/EAN: 9783741182211

Manufactured in Europe, USA, Canada, Australia, Japa

Cover: Foto ©Andreas Hilbeck / pixelio.de

Manufactured and distributed by brebook publishing software (www.brebook.com)

Anonymus

Choice poems and lyrics

CHOICE POEMS

AND

LYRICS

"Poetry is the record of the best and happiest moments of the happiest and best minds."—SHELLEY.

LONDON
WHITTAKER & CO., AVE MARIA LANE
1862

To
WILLIAM WATSON FOSTER, Esq.

OF NEWCASTLE-ON-TYNE,

THIS VOLUME IS DEDICATED

BY HIS SINCERE FRIEND,

THE COMPILER.

PREFACE.

IN compiling this volume an effort has been made to give a salient extract from the works of each poet named, without multiplying quotations from the same author, so as to include in the selection the names of as many authors as the size of the volume would allow. Necessarily, a number of writers have been passed over whose metrical compositions adorn the anthological literature of our country, the size of the book rendering numerous omissions unavoidable. The extracts given from those poets who wrote at a comparatively early period in our own poetic annals, have been chosen with care, so as to avoid the insertion of anything too coarse to be in coincidence with the taste of the present age. Thus the book, it is hoped, will be an acceptable one to be placed in the hands of youth.

For the copyright pieces included, the compiler desires to tender his acknowledgments, not only for the license granted him to print these pieces, but for the polite terms in which, in every instance, both from authors and publishers, the concession was intimated. He wishes particularly to recognize the courtesy of Lady Trevelyan, in placing at his disposal Lord Macaulay's "Ivry," and of Mrs. Moir for her gracefully conveyed assent to the introduction of "Casa Wappy," the exquisite production of the lamented Delta of Blackwood. Truly of this little poem does Mr. Aird (Moir's biographer) say, "Its simple, sobbing, wailing pathos, has drawn more tears of mothers than any other dirge of our day."

The compiler's thanks, too, are pointedly due to Mr. Tennyson, Sir E. Bulwer Lytton, Mr. Kingsley, Professor Aytoun, Mr. Moultrie, and others whose copyright productions confer a lustre on the book which contains them.

Amongst the pieces cited, which will probably

Preface. ix

obtain more than the usual share of admiration, may be named the extract from Mr. Moultrie's "My Brother's Grave," which was originally published in "The Etonian" (a magazine which has long ceased to exist), when the gifted author of the poem was a very young man. Mr. M'Dermot, speaking of it in his "Beauties of Modern Literature," says, after alluding to the tenderness and sweetness of the versification, "After placing before us the deep and still silence of

'That unstartled sleep
The living eye hath never known;'

and terrifying us with the *inania regna* of the ideal world, how sublimely and happily is the following image introduced:—

'The lonely sexton's footstep falls,
In dismal echoes on the walls.'"

No critical panegyric, however, is needed to commend the poem to the attention of its readers. Mr. Waugh's little lyric, "Come whoam to thy childer an' me," taken from his delightful volume of "Poems and Lancashire Songs," is of universal popularity in the district where the Lancashire phrases used are understood, and the true poetry which it contains renders it worthy of world-wide fame.

It is hoped that no apology is required for the lyrical pieces here quoted; all of them are of high merit as poetical compositions, apart from their lyric character.

The compiler sincerely trusts, that the pleasure he has found in his researches to make these selections, may be reflected on the readers of the book.

LIST OF AUTHORS QUOTED.

	Page		Page
ADDISON, Joseph	139	Cook, Eliza	295
Aird, Thomas	52	Cotton, Nathaniel	162
Akenside, Mark	150	Cowley, Abraham	227
Aytoun, W. Edmondstoune	31	Cowper, William	114
		Crabbe, George	218
BAILEY, Philip James	293	Cunningham, Allan	273
Baillie, Joanna	274	Cunningham, John	282
Beattie, James	119		
Blacklock, Thomas	165	DANA, Richard Henry	303
Blair, Robert	155	Davis, Sir John	193
Bloomfield, Robert	91	Denham, John	138
Bruce, Michael	186	Dibdin, Charles	167
Bryant, William Cullen	58	Doane, George W.	302
Burns, Robert	121	Drayton, Michael	174
Byron, Lord	27	Drummond, William	176
		Dryden, John	264
CAMPBELL, Thomas	67	Dyer, John	146
Carew, Thomas	217		
Carlisle, Earl of	189	FALCONER, William	211
Chatterton, Thomas	196	Fergusson, Robert	181
Cibber, Colley	263	Fletcher, Phineas	238
Coleridge, Samuel Taylor	87		
Collins, William	73	GAY, John	230

List of Authors Quoted.

	Page		Page
Goldsmith, Oliver	69	Mickle, William Julius	200
Grahame, James	132	Milton, John	109
Gray, Thomas	77	Moir, David Macbeth	4
		Montgomery, James	105
HABINGTON, William	233	Moore, Thomas	95
Heber, Reginald	251	Motherwell, William	134
Hedderwick, James	296	Moultrie, Rev. John	21
Hemans, Felicia Dorothea	39		
Herbert, George	213	NICOLL, Robert	168
Herrick, Robert	178		
Hogg, James	278	PARNELL, Thomas	206
Howard, H. (E. of Surrey)	216	Patmore Coventry	38
Hunter, Anne	283	Peabody, William O.	300
		Penrose, Thomas	260
JOHNSON, Samuel	152	Poe, Edgar Allan	44
Jonson, Ben	113	Pollok, Robert	190
		Pomfret, John	252
KEN, Thomas	184	Pope, Alexander	142
Kingsley, Rev. Charles	20	Porteus, Beilby	239
		Pringle, Thomas	279
LANGHORNE, John	245	Prior, Matthew	235
Lewis, Matthew Gregory	170	Procter, Adelaide Anne	298
Leyden, John	272		
Logan, John	130	RALEIGH, Sir Walter	259
Longfellow, Henry W.	25	Ramsay, Allan	280
Lovelace, Richard	203	Robinson, Mary	170
Lowell, James Russell	224	Roscommon, Earl of	241
Lyly, John	232		
Lytton, Sir E. Bulwer	15	SCOTT, Sir Walter	62
		Shakspere, William	108
MACAULAY, Lord	10	Shenstone, William	148
Mackay, Charles	290	Shirley, James	175
Marlowe, Christopher	234	Sigourney, Mrs. L. H.	310
Marvell, Andrew	222	Smith, Alexander	287
Mason, William	256	Smith, Charlotte	180
Merrick, James	247	Smollett, Tobias	253

List of Authors Quoted.

	Page		Page
Southey, Robert	97	Watts, Isaac	221
Southwell, Robert	198	Waugh, Edwin	284
Spenser, Edmund	215	White, Henry Kirke	82
Swain, Charles	61	Whitehead, William	157
Swift, Jonathan	209	Whittier, John G.	305
		Willis, Nathaniel P.	308
TANNAHILL, Robert	129	Wilson, Alexander	275
Tennyson, Alfred	1	Wilson, Professor	136
Thomson, James	116	Wither, George	270
Tickell, Thomas	144	Wolfe, Rev. Charles	56
		Wordsworth, William	101
VAUGHAN, Henry	204	Wotton, Sir Henry	192
		Wyatt, Sir Thomas	195
WALTON, Isaac	244		
Warton, Thomas	159	YOUNG, Rev. Edward	93

INDEX . 315

Alfred Tennyson.

Born 1810.

THE MAY QUEEN.

You must wake and call me early, call me early, mother dear ;
To-morrow 'ill be the happiest time of all the glad New-year ;
Of all the glad New-year, mother, the maddest merriest day ;
For I'm to be Queen o' the May, mother, I'm to be Queen o' the May.

There's many a black black eye, they say, but none so bright as mine ;
There's Margaret and Mary, there's Kate and Caroline :
But none so fair as little Alice in all the land they say,
So I'm to be Queen o' the May, mother, I'm to be Queen o' the May.

I sleep so sound all night, mother, that I shall never wake,

If you do not call me loud when the day begins to
  break:
But I must gather knots of flowers, and buds and
  garlands gay,
For I'm to be Queen o' the May, mother, I'm to be
  Queen o' the May.

As I came up the valley whom think ye should I see,
But Robin leaning on the bridge beneath the hazel-tree?
He thought of that sharp look, mother, I gave him
  yesterday,—
But I'm to be Queen o' the May, mother, I'm to be
  Queen o' the May.

He thought I was a ghost, mother, for I was all in
  white,
And I ran by him without speaking, like a flash of
  light.
They call me cruel-hearted, but I care not what they
  say,
For I'm to be Queen o' the May, mother, I'm to be
  Queen o' the May.

They say he's dying all for love, but that can never be.
They say his heart is breaking, mother—what is that
  to me?
There's many a bolder lad 'ill woo me any summer day,
And I'm to be Queen o' the May, mother, I'm to be
  Queen o' the May.

The May Queen.

Little Effie shall go with me to-morrow to the green,
And you'll be there, too, mother, to see me made the
 Queen;
For the shepherd lads on every side 'ill come from far
 away,
And I'm to be Queen o' the May, mother, I'm to be
 Queen o' the May.

The honeysuckle round the porch has wov'n its wavy
 bowers,
And by the meadow-trenches blow the faint sweet
 cuckoo-flowers;
And the wild marsh-marigold shines like fire in swamps
 and hollows gray,
And I'm to be Queen o' the May, mother, I'm to be
 Queen o' the May.

The night-winds come and go, mother, upon the
 meadow-grass,
And the happy stars above them seem to brighten as
 they pass;
There will not be a drop of rain the whole of the live-
 long day,
And I'm to be Queen o' the May, mother, I'm to be
 Queen o' the May.

All the valley, mother, 'ill be fresh and green and
 still,
And the cowslip and the crowfoot are over all the hill,

And the rivulet in the flowery dale 'ill merrily glance
    and play,
For I'm to be Queen o' the May, mother, I'm to be
    Queen o' the May.

So you must wake and call me early, call me early,
    mother dear,
To-morrow 'ill be the happiest time of all the glad
    New-year:
To-morrow 'ill be of all the year the maddest merriest
    day,
For I'm to be Queen o' the May, mother, I'm to be
    Queen o' the May.

David Macbeth Moir.

Born 1798.   Died 1851.

CASA WAPPY.*

AND hast thou sought thy heavenly home,
    Our fond, dear boy—
The realms where sorrow dare not come,
    Where life is joy?
Pure at thy death, as at thy birth,

* The self-appellation of a beloved child.

Thy spirit caught no taint from earth,
Even by its bliss we mete our dearth,
     Casa Wappy!

Despair was in our last farewell,
 As closed thine eye ;
Tears of our anguish may not tell,
 When thou did'st die ;
Words may not paint our grief for thee,
Sighs are but bubbles on the sea
Of our unfathom'd agony,
     Casa Wappy !

Thou wert a vision of delight
 To bless us given ;
Beauty embodied to our sight—
 A type of Heaven :
So dear to us thou wert, thou art
Even less thine own self, than a part
Of mine, and of thy mother's heart,
     Casa Wappy !

Thy bright, brief day knew no decline—
 'Twas cloudless joy ;
Sunrise and night alone were thine,
 Beloved boy !
This morn beheld thee blithe and gay ;
That found thee prostrate in decay ;
And, ere a third shone, clay was clay,
     Casa Wappy !

Gem of our hearth, our household pride,
    Earth's undefiled,
Could love have saved, thou had'st not died,
    Our dear, sweet child!
Humbly we bow to Fate's decree;
Yet had we hoped that Time should see
Thee mourn for us, not us for thee,
              Casa Wappy!

Do what I may, go where I will,
    Thou meet'st my sight;
There dost thou glide before me still—
    A form of light!
I feel thy breath upon my cheek,
I see thee smile, I hear thee speak,
Till oh! my heart is like to break,
              Casa Wappy!

Methinks, thou smil'st before me now,
    With glance of stealth;
The hair thrown back from thy full brow
    In buoyant health:
I see thine eyes' deep violet light,
Thy dimpled cheek carnation'd bright,
Thy clasping arms so round and white,
              Casa Wappy!

The nursery shows thy pictured wall,
    Thy bat, thy bow,

Thy cloak and bonnet, club and ball;
    But where art thou?
A corner holds thine empty chair;
Thy play-things idly scattered there,
But speak to us of our despair,
                    Casa Wappy!

Even to the last, thy every word—
    To glad—to grieve—
Was sweet, as sweetest song of bird
    On summer's eve;
In outward beauty undecay'd,
Death o'er thy spirit cast no shade,
And, like the rainbow, thus did'st fade,
                    Casa Wappy!

We mourn for thee, when blind blank night
    The chamber fills;
We pine for thee, when morn's first light
    Reddens the hills;
The sun, the moon, the stars, the sea,
All—to the wall-flower and wild pea—
Are changed: we saw the world thro' thee,
                    Casa Wappy!

And though, perchance, a smile may gleam
    Of casual mirth,
It doth not own, whate'er may seem,
    An inward birth:

We miss thy small step on the stair;
We miss thee at thine evening prayer;
All day we miss thee—everywhere—
    Casa Wappy!

Snows muffled earth when thou did'st go,
 In life's spring-bloom,
Down to the appointed house below—
 The silent tomb.
But now the green leaves of the tree,
The cuckoo, and " the busy bee,"
Return; but with them bring not thee,
    Casa Wappy!

'Tis so; but can it be—(while flowers
 Revive again)—
Man's doom, in death that we and ours
 For aye remain?
Oh! can it be, that, o'er the grave,
The grass renew'd should yearly wave,
Yet God forget our child to save?—
    Casa Wappy!

It cannot be; for were it so
 Thus man could die,
Life were a mockery—Thought were woe—
 And Truth a lie—
Heaven were a coinage of the brain—
Religion frenzy—Virtue vain—

And all our hopes to meet again,
                Casa Wappy!

Then be to us, O dear, lost child!
    With beam of love,
A star, death's uncongenial wild
    Smiling above!
Soon, soon, thy little feet have trod
The skyward path, the seraph's road,
That led thee back from man to God,
                Casa Wappy!

Yet 'tis sweet balm to our despair,
    Fond, fairest boy,
That Heaven is God's, and thou art there,
    With him in joy!
There, past are death and all its woes,
There, beauty's stream for ever flows,
And pleasure's day no sunset knows,
                Casa Wappy!

Farewell, then—for a while, farewell—
    Pride of my heart!
It cannot be that long we dwell,
    Thus torn apart:
Time's shadows like the shuttle flee;
And, dark howe'er life's night may be,
Beyond the grave I'll meet with thee,
                Casa Wappy!

Lord Macaulay.

Born 1800. Died 1859.

IVRY.*

Now glory to the Lord of Hosts, from whom all glories are !
And glory to our sovereign liege, King Henry of Navarre !
Now let there be the merry sound of music and of dance,
Through thy corn-fields green, and sunny vines, oh pleasant land of France !
And thou, Rochelle, our own Rochelle, proud city of the waters,
Again let rapture light the eyes of all thy mourning daughters.
As thou wert constant in our ills, be joyous in our joy,
For cold, and stiff, and still are they who wrought thy walls annoy.
Hurrah ! hurrah ! a single field hath turned the chance of war,
Hurrah ! hurrah ! for Ivry, and Henry of Navarre.

Oh ! how our hearts were beating, when, at the dawn of day,

* The battle of Ivry was won by Henry IV., King of France and Navarre, over the leaders of the League in 1590.

We saw the army of the League drawn out in long
    array
With all its priest-led citizens, and all its rebel peers,
And Appenzel's stout infantry, and Egmont's Flemish
    spears.
There rode the brood of false Lorraine, the curses of
    our land ;
And dark Mayenne was in the midst, a truncheon in his
    hand :
And, as we looked on them, we thought of Seine's
    empurpled flood,
And good Coligni's hoary hair all dabbled with his
    blood ;
And we cried unto the living God, who rules the fate
    of war,
To fight for his own holy name, and Henry of Navarre.

The king is come to marshal us, in all his armour drest,
And he has bound a snow-white plume upon his gallant
    crest.
He looked upon his people, and a tear was in his eye ;
He looked upon the traitors, and his glance was stern
    and high.
Right graciously he smiled on us, as rolled from wing to
    wing,
Down all our line, a deafening shout, "God save our
    Lord the King."
" An if my standard-bearer fall, as fall full well he may,
For never saw I promise yet of such a bloody fray,

Press where ye see my white plume shine, amidst the
    ranks of war,
And be your oriflamme to-day, the helmet of Navarre."

Hurrah! the foes are moving. Hark to the mingled
    din,
Of fife, and steed, and trump, and drum, and roaring
    culverin.
The fiery Duke is pricking fast across St. André's
    plain,
With all the hireling chivalry of Guelders and Almayne.
Now by the lips of those ye love, fair gentlemen of
    France,
Charge for the golden lilies,—upon them with the lance.
A thousand spurs are striking deep, a thousand spears
    in rest,
A thousand knights are pressing close behind the snow-
    white crest;
And in they burst, and on they rushed, while, like a
    guiding star,
Amidst the thickest carnage blazed the helmet of
    Navarre.

Now, God be praised, the day is ours. Mayenne hath
    turned his rein;
D'Aumale hath cried for quarter. The Flemish count is
    slain.
Their ranks are breaking like thin clouds before a Biscay
    gale;

The field is heaped with bleeding steeds, and flags, and
    cloven mail.
And then we thought on vengeance, and, all along our
    van,
"Remember Saint Bartholomew," was passed from man
    to man.
But out spake gentle Henry, "No Frenchman is my foe:
Down, down, with every foreigner, but let your brethren
    go."
Oh! was there ever such a knight, in friendship or in
    war,
As our Sovereign Lord, King Henry, the soldier of
    Navarre?

Right well fought all the Frenchmen who fought for
    France to-day;
And many a lordly banner God gave them for a prey.
But we of the religion have borne us best in fight;
And the good Lord of Rosny hath ta'en the cornet
    white.
Our own true Maximilian the cornet white hath ta'en,
The cornet white with crosses black, the flag of false
    Lorraine.
Up with it high; unfurl it wide; that all the host may
    know
How God hath humbled the proud house which wrought
    his church such woe.
Then on the ground, while trumpets sound their loudest
    point of war,

Fling the red shreds, a footcloth meet for Henry of
    Navarre.

Ho! maidens of Vienna; Ho! matrons of Lucerne;
Weep, weep, and rend your hair for those who never
    shall return.
Ho! Philip, send, for charity, thy Mexican pistoles,
That Antwerp monks may sing a mass for thy poor
    spearmen's souls,
Ho! gallant nobles of the League, look that your arms
    be bright;
Ho! burghers of Saint Genevieve, keep watch and ward
    to-night.
For our God hath crushed the tyrant, our God hath
    raised the slave,
And mocked the counsel of the wise, and the valour of
    the brave.
Then glory to his holy name, from whom all glories are;
And glory to our Sovereign Lord, King Henry of
    Navarre.

Sir Edward Bulwer Lytton.

Born 1805.

FROM THE LAST DAYS OF QUEEN ELIZABETH.

Rise from thy bloody grave,
  Thou soft Medusa of the Fated Line,*
Whose evil beauty looked to death the brave ;—
  Discrowned Queen, around whose passionate shame
Terror and Grief the palest flowers entwine,
  That ever veiled the ruins of a Name
With the sweet parasites of song divine !—
    Arise, sad Ghost, arise,
  And, if Revenge outlive the Tomb,
Thou art avenged—Behold the doomer brought to doom !
  Lo, where thy mighty Murderess lies,
    The sleepless couch—the sunless room,—
  And, quelled the eagle-eye and lion mien,
  The woe-worn shadow of the Titan Queen !

There, sorrow-stricken, to the ground,
  Alike by night and day,

* Mary, Queen of Scots. "Soft Medusa" is an expression strikingly applied to her in her own day.

The heart's-blood from the inward wound
   Ebbs silently away.
And oft she turns from face to face,
   A sharp and eager gaze,
As if the memory sought to trace
The sign of some lost dwelling-place
   Beloved in happier days;
     Ah, what the clue supplies
In the cold vigil of a hireling's eyes?
Ah, sad in childless age to weep alone,
   And start and gaze, to find no sorrow save our own!
O Soul, thou speedest to thy rest away,
   But not upon the pinions of the dove;
When death draws nigh, how miserable they
   Who have outlived all love!
As on the solemn verge of Night
   Lingers a weary Moon,
She wanes, the last of every glorious light
   That bathed with splendour her majestic noon:—
The stately stars that clustering o'er the isle
   Lull'd into glittering rest the subject sea;—
Gone the great Masters of Italian wile
   False to the world beside, but true to thee!—
Burleigh, the subtlest builder of thy fame,—
   The gliding craft of winding Walsingham;—
   They who exalted yet before thee bowed;—
And that more dazzling chivalry—the Band
That made thy Court a Faëry Land,
In which thou wert enshrined to reign alone—

The Gloriana of the Diamond Throne ;—
 All gone,—and left thee sad amidst the cloud!
* * * * *
Call back the gorgeous past!
 Lo, England white-robed for a holiday!
While, choral to the clarion's kingly blast,
 Peals shout on shout along the Virgin's way,
 As through the swarming streets rolls on the long array.
Mary is dead!—Look from your fire-won homes,
 Exulting Martyrs!—on the mount shall rest
Truth's ark at last! the avenging Lutheran comes
 And clasps THE BOOK ye died for to her breast!*
With her, the flower of all the Land,
 The high-born gallants ride,
And ever nearest of the band,
With watchful eye and ready hand,
 Young Dudley's form of pride!†
Ah, ev'n in that exulting hour,
Love half allures the soul from Power,—
And blushes, half suppressed, betray
 The woman's hope and fear ;
Like blooms which in the early May

* "When Queen Elizabeth was conducted through London amidst the joyful acclamations of her subjects, a boy, who personated Truth, was let down from one of the triumphal arches, and presented to her a copy of the Bible. She received the book with the most gracious deportment, and placed it next her bosom."— *Hume*.

† Robert Dudley, afterwards the Leicester of doubtful fame, attended Elizabeth in her passage to the Tower.

Bud forth beneath a timorous ray,
   And mark the mellowing year.
While steals the sweetest of all worship paid
   Less to the monarch than the maid,
      Melodious on the ear!

   *   *   *   *   *

Call back the gorgeous Past!
   Where, bright and broadening to the main,
      Rolls on the scornful River,—
   Stout hearts beat high on Tilbury's plain,—
      Our Marathon for ever!
No breeze above, but on the mast
The pennon shook as with the blast.
Forth from the cloud the day-god strode;
O'er bristling helms the splendour glowed,—
Leapt the loud joy from Earth to Heaven,
As, through the ranks asunder riven,
      The Warrior-Woman rode!
   Hark, thrilling through the arméd line
      The martial accents ring,
"Though mine the Woman's form—yet mine,
   The Heart of England's King!" *
Woe to the Island and the Maid!
The Pope has preached the new crusade,
His sons have caught the fiery zeal;—
The Monks are merry in Castile;

---

* "I know I have but the body of a weak and feeble woman, but I have the heart of a king, and of a king of England too."—*Queen Elizabeth's Harangue at Tilbury Camp.*

Bold Parma on the Main;
And through the deep-exulting sweep
The Thunder-Steeds of Spain.*
What meteor rides the sulphurous gale?
The Flames have caught the giant sail!
Fierce Drake† is grappling prow to prow;
God and St. George for Victory now!
Death in the Battle and the Wind—
Carnage before and Storm behind—
Wild shrieks are heard above the hurtling roar
By Orkney's rugged strands, and Erin's ruthless shore.
Joy to the Island and the Maid!
Pope Sixtus wept the Last Crusade!
His sons consumed before his zeal,—
The Monks are woeful in Castile;
Your Monument the Main,
The glaive and gale record your tale,
Ye Thunder-Steeds of Spain!

* *Thunder-steeds*, the Spanish ships.
† Sir Francis Drake, who acted as Vice-Admiral in the action against the Spanish Armada.

Rev. Charles Kingsley.

Born 1819.

THE THREE FISHERS.

Three fishers went sailing away to the West,
  Away to the West as the sun went down;
Each thought on the woman who loved him the best,
  And the children stood watching them out of the
    town;
  For men must work, and women must weep,
  And there's little to earn, and many to keep,
    Though the harbour bar be moaning.

Three wives sat up in the light-house tower,
  And they trimmed the lamps as the sun went down;
They looked at the squall, and they looked at the
    shower,
  And the night-rack came rolling up ragged and
    brown.
  But men must work, and women must weep,
  Though storms be sudden, and waters deep,
    And the harbour bar be moaning.

Three corpses lay out on the shining sands
  In the morning gleam as the tide went down,

And the women are weeping and wringing their hands
For those who will never come home to the town ;
For men must work, and women must weep,
And the sooner it's over, the sooner to sleep ;
And good-bye to the bar and its moaning.

Rev. John Moultrie.

Born 1799.

FROM MY BROTHER'S GRAVE.

Beneath the chancel's hallowed stone,
    Exposed to every rustic tread,
To few, save rustic mourners, known,
    My brother, is thy lowly bed.
Few words upon the rough stone 'graven,
    Thy name, thy birth, thy youth declare,
Thy innocence, thy hopes of heaven,
    In simplest phrase recorded there.
No 'scutcheons shine, no banners wave,
In mockery o'er my brother's grave.

The place is silent ; rarely sound
Is heard those ancient walls around ;

Nor mirthful voice of friends that meet,
Discoursing in the public street;
Nor hum of business, dull and loud,
Nor murmur of the passing crowd,
Nor soldier's drum, nor trumpet's swell,
From neighbouring fort or citadel;
No sound of human toil or strife,
To death's lone dwelling speaks of life,
Nor breaks the silence, still and deep,
  Where thou, beneath thy burial stone
Art laid in that unstartled sleep
  The living eye hath never known.
The lonely sexton's footstep falls
In dismal echoes on the walls,
As, slowly pacing through the aisle,
  He sweeps the unholy dust away,
And cobwebs, which must not defile
  Their windows on the Sabbath day;
And, passing through the central nave,
Treads lightly on my brother's grave.

But when the sweet-toned Sabbath-chime,
  Pouring its music on the breeze,
Proclaims the well-known holy time
  Of prayer, and thanks, and bended knees;
When rustic crowds devoutly meet,
  And lips and hearts to God are given,
And souls enjoy oblivion sweet,
  Of earthly ills in thought of Heaven;

My Brother's Grave.

What voice of calm and solemn tone
Is heard above thy burial-stone?
What form in priestly meek array
Beside the altar kneels to pray?
What holy hands are lifted up
To bless the sacramental cup?
Full well I know that reverend form,
   And if a voice could reach the dead,
Those tones would reach thee, though the worm,
   My brother, makes thy heart his bed;
That sire who thy existence gave,
Now stands beside thy lowly grave.

It is not long since thou wert wont
   Within these sacred walls to kneel;
This altar, that baptismal font,
   These stones which now thy dust conceal,
The sweet tones of the Sabbath bell,
   Were holiest objects to thy soul,
On them thy spirit loved to dwell,
   Untainted by the world's control.
My brother, those were happy days,
   When thou and I were children yet;
How fondly memory still surveys
   Those scenes the heart can ne'er forget!
My soul was then as thine is now,
   Unstained by sin—unstung by pain;
Peace smiled on each unclouded brow,
   Mine ne'er will be so calm again.

How blithely then we hailed the ray
Which ushered in the Sabbath-day!
How lightly then our footsteps trod
Yon pathway to the house of God!
For souls in which no dark offence
Hath sullied childhood's innocence,
Best meet the pure and hallowed shrine,
Which guiltier bosoms own divine.
I feel not now as then I felt,
   The sunshine of my heart is o'er;
The spirit now is changed which dwelt
   Within me, in the days before.
But thou wert snatched, my brother, hence,
In all thy guileless innocence;
One Sabbath saw thee bend the knee
In reverential piety;
For childish faults forgiveness crave,
The next beamed brightly on thy grave!
The crowd, of which thou late wert one,
Now thronged across thy burial stone;
Rude footsteps trampled on the spot
Where thou liest mouldering and forgot;
And some few gentler bosoms wept,
In silence where my brother slept.

I stood not by thy feverish bed,
   I looked not on thy glazing eye,
Nor gently lulled thy aching head,
   Nor viewed thy dying agony;

I felt not what my parents felt,
    The doubt, the terror, the distress;
Nor vainly for my brother knelt,
    My soul was spared that wretchedness.
One sentence told me in a breath
My brother's illness, and his death!

H. Wadsworth Longfellow.

Born 1807.

THE WARDEN OF THE CINQUE PORTS.*

A mist was driving down the British Channel,
    The day was just begun,
And through the window-panes, on floor and panel,
    Streamed the red autumn sun.

It glanced on flowing flag and rippling pennon,
    And the white sails of ships;
And, from the frowning rampart, the black cannon
    Hailed it with feverish lips.

Sandwich and Romney, Hastings, Hythe and Dover,
    Were all alert that day,
To see the French war-steamers speeding over,
    When the fog cleared away.

    * The Duke of Wellington.

Sullen and silent, and like couchant lions,
    Their cannon through the night,
Holding their breath, had watched in grim defiance
    The sea-coast opposite.

And now they roared at drum-beat from their stations
    On every citadel;
Each answering each with morning salutations
    That all was well.

And down the coast, all taking up the burden,
    Replied the distant forts,
As if to summon from his sleep the Warden
    And Lord of the Cinque Ports.

Him shall no sunshine from the fields of azure,
    No drum-beat from the wall,
No morning-gun from the black fort's embrasure
    Awaken with their call.

No more surveying with an eye impartial
    The long line of the coast,
Shall the gaunt figure of the old Field-Marshal
    Be seen upon his post.

For in the night, unseen, a single warrior,
    In sombre harness mailed,
Dreaded of man, and surnamed the Destroyer,
    The rampart-wall has scaled.

He passed into the chamber of the sleeper,
    The dark and silent room ;
And as he entered, darker grew and deeper
    The silence and the gloom.

He did not pause to parley or dissemble,
    But smote the Warden hoar ;
Ah ! what a blow ! that made all England tremble,
    And groan from shore to shore.

Meanwhile, without the surly cannon waited,
    The sun rose bright o'er head ;
Nothing in Nature's aspect intimated
    That a great man was dead !

Lord Byron.

Born 1788. Died 1824.

THE NIGHT BEFORE THE BATTLE OF WATERLOO.

There was a sound of revelry by night,
And Belgium's capital had gathered then
Her Beauty and her Chivalry, and bright
The lamps shone o'er fair women and brave men ;
A thousand hearts beat happily ; and when
Music arose with its voluptuous swell,

Soft eyes looked love to eyes which spake again,
And all went merry as a marriage-bell ;
But hush ! hark ! a deep sound strikes like a rising knell !

Did ye not hear it ?—No ; 't was but the wind,
Or the car rattling o'er the stony street ;
On with the dance ! let joy be unconfined ;
No sleep till morn when Youth and Pleasure meet
To chase the glowing Hours with flying feet—
But, hark !—that heavy sound breaks in once more,
As if the clouds its echo would repeat ;
And nearer, clearer, deadlier than before !
Arm ! Arm ! it is—it is—the cannon's opening roar !

Within a windowed niche of that high hall
Sate Brunswick's fated chieftain ; he did hear
That sound the first amidst the festival,
And caught its tone with Death's prophetic ear ;
And when they smiled because he deemed it near,
His heart more truly knew that peal too well
Which stretched his father on a bloody bier,
And roused the vengeance blood alone could quell :
He rushed into the field, and, foremost fighting, fell.

Ah ! then and there was hurrying to and fro,
And gathering tears, and tremblings of distress,
And cheeks all pale, which but an hour ago
Blushed at the praise of their own loveliness ;
And there were sudden partings, such as press

The life from out young hearts, and choking sighs
Which ne'er might be repeated; who could guess
If ever more should meet those mutual eyes,
Since upon nights so sweet such awful morn could rise?

And there was mounting in hot haste: the steed,
The mustering squadron, and the clattering car,
Went pouring forward with impetuous speed,
And swiftly forming in the ranks of war;
And the deep thunder peal on peal afar;
And near, the beat of the alarming drum
Roused up the soldier ere the morning star;
While thronged the citizens with terror dumb,
Or whispering, with white lips—"The foe! They come! They come!"

And wild and high the "Cameron's gathering" rose!
The war-note of Lochiel, which Albyn's hills
Have heard, and heard, too, have her Saxon foes:—
How in the noon of night that pibroch thrills,
Savage and shrill! But with the breath which fills
Their mountain-pipe, so fill the mountaineers
With the fierce native daring which instils
The stirring memory of a thousand years,
And Evan's, Donald's fame rings in each clansman's ears!

And Ardennes waves above them her green leaves,
Dewy with nature's tear-drops, as they pass,

Grieving, if aught inanimate e'er grieves,
Over the unreturning brave,—alas !
Ere evening to be trodden like the grass
Which now beneath them, but above shall grow
In its next verdure, when this fiery mass
Of living valour, rolling on the foe
And burning with high hope, shall moulder cold and low.

Last noon beheld them full of lusty life,
Last eve in Beauty's circle proudly gay,
The midnight brought the signal-sound of strife,
The morn the marshalling in arms,—the day
Battle's magnificently-stern array !
The thunder-clouds close o'er it, which when rent
The earth is covered thick with other clay,
Which her own clay shall cover, heaped and pent,
Rider and horse,—friend, foe, in one red burial blent !

W. Edmondstoune Aytoun.

Born 1813.

THE BURIAL-MARCH OF DUNDEE.*

SOUND the fife, and cry the slogan—
 Let the pibroch shake the air
With its wild triumphal music,
 Worthy of the freight we bear.
Let the ancient hills of Scotland
 Hear once more the battle-song
Swell within their glens and valleys
 As the clansmen march along!
Never from the field of combat,
 Never from the deadly fray,
Was a nobler trophy carried
 Than we bring with us to-day—
Never, since the valiant Douglas
 On his dauntless bosom bore
Good King Robert's heart—the priceless—
 To our dear Redeemer's shore!
Lo! we bring with us the hero—
 Lo! we bring the conquering Græme,
Crowned as best beseems a victor
 From the altar of his fame;

---

* John Graham of Claverhouse, Viscount Dundee, was killed at the battle of Killiecrankie in Scotland.

Fresh and bleeding from the battle
　　Whence his spirit took its flight,
Midst the crashing charge of squadrons,
　　And the thunder of the fight!
Strike, I say, the notes of triumph,
　　As we march o'er moor and lea!
Is there any here will venture
　　To bewail our dead Dundee?
Let the widows of the traitors
　　Weep until their eyes are dim!
Wail ye may full well for Scotland—
　　Let none dare to mourn for him!
See! above his glorious body
　　Lies the royal banner's fold—
See! his valiant blood is mingled—
　　With its crimson and its gold—
See how calm he looks, and stately,
　　Like a warrior on his shield,
Waiting till the flush of morning
　　Breaks along the battle-field!
See—Oh never more, my comrades,
　　Shall we see that falcon eye
Redden with its inward lightning,
　　As the hour of fight drew nigh!
Never shall we hear the voice that
　　Clearer than the trumpet's call,
Bade us strike for King and Country,
　　Bade us win the field, or fall!

The Burial-March of Dundee.

On the heights of Killiecrankie
   Yester-morn our army lay:
Slowly rose the mist in columns
   From the river's broken way;
Hoarsely roared the swollen torrent,
   And the Pass was wrapt in gloom,
When the clansmen rose together
   From their lair amidst the broom.
Then we belted on our tartans,
   And our bonnets down we drew,
And we felt our broadswords' edges,
   And we proved them to be true;
And we prayed the prayer of soldiers,
   And we cried the gathering-cry,
And we clasped the hands of kinsmen,
   And we swore to do or die!
Then our leader rode before us
   On his war-horse black as night—
Well the Cameronian rebels
   Knew that charger in the fight!—
And a cry of exultation
   From the bearded warriors rose;
For we loved the house of Claver'se,
   And we thought of good Montrose.
But he raised his hand for silence—
   "Soldiers! I have sworn a vow:
Ere the evening star shall glisten
   On Schehallion's lofty brow,
Either we shall rest in triumph,

Or another of the Græmes
Shall have died in battle-harness
  For his Country and King James!
Think upon the Royal Martyr—
  Think of what his race endure—
Think of him whom butchers murdered
  On the field of Magus Muir:—
By his sacred blood I charge ye,
  By the ruined hearth and shrine—
By the blighted hopes of Scotland,
  By your injuries and mine—
Strike this day as if the anvil
  Lay beneath your blows the while,
Be they covenanting traitors,
  Or the brood of false Argyle!
Strike! and drive the trembling rebels
  Backwards o'er the stormy Forth;
Let them tell their pale Convention
  How they fared within the North.
Let them tell that Highland honour
  Is not to be bought nor sold,
That we scorn their prince's anger
  As we loathe his foreign gold.
Strike! and when the fight is over,
  If ye look in vain for me,
Where the dead are lying thickest,
  Search for him that was Dundee!"

Loudly then the hills re-echoed

With our answer to his call,
But a deeper echo sounded
In the bosoms of us all.
For the lands of wide Breadalbane,
Not a man who heard him speak
Would that day have left the battle.
Burning eye and flushing cheek
Told the clansmen's fierce emotion,
And they harder drew their breath;
For their souls were strong within them,
Stronger than the grasp of death.
Soon we heard a challenge-trumpet
Sounding in the Pass below,
And the distant tramp of horses,
And the voices of the foe:
Down we crouched amid the bracken,
Till the Lowland ranks drew near,
Panting like the hounds in summer,
When they scent the stately deer.
From the dark defile emerging,
Next we saw the squadrons come,
Leslie's foot and Leven's troopers
Marching to the tuck of drum;
Through the scattered wood of birches,
O'er the broken ground and heath,
Wound the long battalion slowly,
Till they gained the plain beneath;
Then we bounded from our covert.—
Judge how looked the Saxons then,

When they saw the rugged mountain
    Start to life with armèd men!
Like a tempest down the ridges
    Swept the hurricane of steel,
Rose the slogan of Macdonald—
    Flashed the broadsword of Lochiel!
Vainly sped the withering volley
    'Mongst the foremost of our band—
On we poured until we met them,
    Foot to foot, and hand to hand.
Horse and man went down like drift-wood
    When the floods are black at Yule,
And their carcasses are whirling
    In the Garry's deepest pool.
Horse and man went down before us—
    Living foe there tarried none
On the field of Killiecrankie,
    When that stubborn fight was done!

And the evening star was shining
    On Schehallion's distant head,
When we wiped our bloody broadswords,
    And returned to count the dead.
There we found him gashed and gory,
    Stretched upon the cumbered plain,
As he told us where to seek him,
    In the thickest of the slain.
And a smile was on his visage,
    For within his dying ear

Pealed the joyful note of triumph,
   And the clansmen's clamorous cheer:
So, amidst the battle's thunder,
   Shot, and steel, and scorching flame,
In the glory of his manhood
   Passed the spirit of the Græme!

Open wide the vaults of Atholl,
   Where the bones of heroes rest—
Open wide the hallowed portals
   To receive another guest!
Last of Scots, and last of freemen—
   Last of all that dauntless race,
Who would rather die unsullied
   Than outlive the land's disgrace!
O thou lion-hearted warrior!
   Reck not of the after-time:
Honour may be deemed dishonour,
   Loyalty be called a crime.
Sleep in peace with kindred ashes
   Of the noble and the true,
Hands that never failed their country,
   Hearts that never baseness knew.
Sleep!—and till the latest trumpet
   Wakes the dead from earth and sea,
Scotland shall not boast a braver
   Chieftain than our own Dundee!

Coventry Patmore.
Born 1823.

THE WIFE'S TRAGEDY.

Man must be pleased; but him to please
  Is woman's pleasure; down the gulf
Of his condoled necessities
  She casts her best, she flings herself.
How often flings for nought! and yokes
  Her heart to an icicle or whim,
Whose each impatient word provokes
  Another, not from her, but him;
While she, too gentle even to force
  His penitence by kind replies,
Waits by, expecting his remorse,
  With pardon in her pitying eyes;
And if he once, by shame oppressed,
  A comfortable word confers,
She leans and weeps against his breast,
  And seems to think the sin was hers;
And whilst his love has any life,
  Or any eye to see her charms,
At any time, she's still his wife,
  Dearly devoted to his arms;
She loves with love that cannot tire;
  And when, ah woe, she loves alone,
Through passionate duty love flames higher,
  As grass grows taller round a stone.

Felicia Dorothea Hemans.

Born 1793. Died 1835.

MARGUERITE OF FRANCE.*

The Moslem spears were gleaming
　　Round Damietta's towers,
Though a Christian banner from her wall
　　Waved free its lily-flowers.
Ay, proudly did the banner wave,
　　As queen of earth and air ;
But faint hearts throbbed beneath its folds
　　In anguish and despair.

Deep, deep in Paynim dungeon
　　Their kingly chieftain lay,
And low on many an eastern field
　　Their knighthood's best array.
'Twas mournful when at feasts they met,
　　The wine-cup round to send ;

---

* Queen of St Louis. Whilst besieged by the Turks in Damletta, during the captivity of the king her husband, she there gave birth to a son, whom she named Tristan, in commemoration of her misfortunes. Information being conveyed to her, that the knights intrusted with the defence of the city had resolved on capitulation, she had them summoned to her apartment; and by her heroic words, so wrought upon their spirits, that they vowed to defend her and the Cross to the last extremity.

For each that touched it silently
    Then missed a gallant friend!

And mournful was their vigil
    On the beleaguered wall,
And dark their slumber, dark with dreams
    Of slow defeat and fall.
Yet a few hearts of chivalry
    Rose high to breast the storm,
And one—of all the loftiest there—
    Thrilled in a woman's form.

A woman meekly bending
    O'er the slumber of her child,
With her soft, sad eyes of weeping love,
    As the Virgin Mother's mild.
Oh! roughly cradled was thy babe,
    Midst the clash of spear and lance,
And a strange, wild bower was thine, young [queen!
    Fair Marguerite of France!

A dark and vaulted chamber,
    Like a scene for wizard-spell,
Deep in the Saracenic gloom
    Of the warrior citadel;
And there midst arms the couch was spread,
    And with banners curtained o'er,
For the daughter of the minstrel-land
    The gay Provençal shore!

For the bright queen of St. Louis,
  The star of court and hall!
But the deep strength of the gentle heart
  Wakes to the tempest's call!
Her lord was in the Paynim's hold,
  His soul with grief oppressed,
Yet calmly lay the desolate,
  With her young babe on her breast!

There were voices in the city,
  Voices of wrath and fear—
"The walls grow weak, the strife is vain—
  We will not perish here!
Yield! yield! and let the Crescent gleam
  O'er tower and bastion high!
Our distant homes are beautiful—
  We stay not here to die!"

They bore those fearful tidings
  To the sad queen where she lay—
They told a tale of wavering hearts,
  Of treason and dismay:
The blood rushed through her pearly cheek,
  The sparkle to her eye—
"Now call me hither those recreant knights
  From the bands of Italy!"*

---

* The proposal to capitulate is attributed by the French historian to the Knights of Pisa.

Then through the vaulted chambers
  Stern iron footsteps rang;
And heavily the sounding floor
  Gave back the sabre's clang.
They stood around her—steel-clad men,
  Moulded for storm and fight,
But they quailed before the loftier soul
  In that pale aspect bright.

Yes! as before the falcon shrinks
  The bird of meaner wing,
So shrank they from the imperial glance
  Of her—that fragile thing!
And her flute-like voice rose clear and high
  Through the din of arms around—
Sweet, and yet stirring to the soul,
  As a silver clarion's sound.

"The honour of the Lily
  Is in your hands to keep,
And the banner of the Cross, for Him
  Who died on Calvary's steep;
And the city which for Christian prayer
  Hath heard the holy bell—
And is it *these* your hearts would yield
  To the godless infidel?

"Then bring me here a breastplate
  And a helm, before ye fly,

And I will gird my woman's form,
    And on the ramparts die!
And the boy whom I have borne for woe,
    But never for disgrace,
Shall go within mine arms to death
    Meet for his royal race.

"Look on him as he slumbers
    In the shadow of the lance!
Then go, and with the Cross forsake
    The princely babe of France!
But tell your homes ye left *one* heart
    To perish undefiled;
A woman, and a queen, to guard
    Her honour and her child!"

Before her words they thrilled, like leaves
    When winds are in the wood;
And a deepening murmur told of men
    Roused to a loftier mood,
And her babe awoke to flashing swords,
    Unsheathed in many a hand,
As they gathered round the helpless One,
    Again a noble band!

"We are thy warriors, lady!
    True to the Cross and thee;
The spirit of thy kindling words
    On every sword shall be!

Rest, with thy fair child on thy breast!
Rest—we will guard thee well!
St. Denis for the Lily-flower
And the Christian citadel!"

Edgar Allan Poe.

Born 1811. Died 1849.

THE RAVEN.

ONCE upon a midnight dreary, while I pondered, weak and weary,
Over many a quaint and curious volume of forgotten lore—
While I nodded, nearly napping, suddenly there came a tapping,
As of some one gently rapping, rapping at my chamber door.
"'Tis some visitor," I muttered, "tapping at my chamber door—
   Only this, and nothing more."

II.

Ah, distinctly I remember it was in the bleak December,

And each separate dying ember wrought its ghost upon
the floor.
Eagerly I wished the morrow ;—vainly I had sought to
borrow
From my books surcease of sorrow— sorrow for the lost
Lenore—
For the rare and radiant maiden whom the angels name
Lenore—
    Nameless here for evermore.

III.

And the silken sad uncertain rustling of each purple
curtain
Thrilled me—filled me with fantastic terrors never felt
before ;
So that now, to still the beating of my heart, I stood
repeating,
" 'Tis some visitor entreating entrance at my chamber
door—
Some late visitor entreating entrance at my chamber
door ;
    This it is, and nothing more."

IV.

Presently my soul grew stronger ; hesitating then no
longer,
" Sir," said I, " or Madam, truly your forgiveness I
implore ;
But the fact is, I was napping, and so gently you came
rapping,

And so faintly you came tapping, tapping at my chamber
    door,
That I scarce was sure I heard you:"—here I opened
    wide the door;——
        Darkness there, and nothing more.

v.

Deep into that darkness peering, long I stood there
    wondering, fearing,
Doubting, dreaming dreams no mortals ever dared to
    dream before;
But the silence was unbroken, and the stillness gave
    no token,
And the only word there spoken was the whispered
    word, "Lenore?"
This I whispered, and an echo murmured back the
    word, "Lenore!"
        Merely this, and nothing more.

vi.

Back into the chamber turning, all my soul within me
    burning,
Soon again I heard a tapping something louder than
    before.
"Surely," said I, "surely that is something at my win-
    dow lattice;
Let me see, then, what thereat is, and this mystery
    explore—

Let my heart be still a moment, and this mystery explore :—
'Tis the wind and nothing more."

VII.

Open here I flung the shutter, when with many a flirt
and flutter,
In there stepped a stately Raven of the saintly days of
yore.
Not the least obeisance made he; not a minute stopped
or stayed he;
But, with mien of lord or lady, perched above my
chamber door—
Perched upon a bust of Pallas, just above my chamber
door—
Perched, and sat, and nothing more.

VIII.

Then this ebony bird beguiling my sad fancy into
smiling,
By the grave and stern decorum of the countenance it
wore,
"Though thy crest be shorn and shaven, thou," I said,
"art sure no craven,
Ghastly, grim, and ancient Raven, wandering from the
Nightly shore—
Tell me what thy lordly name is on the Night's
Plutonian shore!"
Quoth the Raven, "Nevermore."

IX.

Much I marvelled this ungainly fowl to hear discourse
    so plainly,
Though its answer little meaning—little relevancy bore;
For we cannot help agreeing that no living human being
Ever yet was blessed with seeing bird above his chamber
    door—
Bird or beast upon the sculptured bust above his chamber
    door,
        With such name as " Nevermore."

X.

But the Raven, sitting lonely on that placid bust, spoke
    only
That one word, as if his soul in that one word he did
    outpour.
Nothing farther then he uttered; not a feather then he
    fluttered—
Till I scarcely more than muttered, " Other friends
    have flown before—
On the morrow *he* will leave me, as my Hopes have
    flown before."
        Then the bird said, " Nevermore."

XI.

Startled at the stillness broken by reply so aptly spoken,
" Doubtless," said I, " what it utters is its only stock
    and store,

Caught from some unhappy master, whom unmerciful
    Disaster
Followed fast and followed faster, till his songs one
    burden bore—
Till the dirges of his Hope that melancholy burden bore,
            Of 'Never—nevermore.'"

XII.

But the Raven still beguiling all my sad soul into
    smiling,
Straight I wheeled a cushioned seat in front of bird, and
    bust, and door;
Then, upon the velvet sinking, I betook myself to
    linking
Fancy unto fancy, thinking what this ominous bird of
    yore—
What this grim, ungainly, ghastly, gaunt, and ominous
    bird of yore,
            Meant in croaking, "Nevermore."

XIII.

This I sat engaged in guessing, but no syllable ex-
    pressing
To the fowl, whose fiery eyes now burned into my
    bosom's core;
This and more I sat divining, with my head at ease re-
    clining
On the cushion's velvet lining that the lamp-light
    gloated o'er,

But whose velvet violet lining with the lamp-light
   gloating o'er,
      She shall press, ah, nevermore!

XIV.

Then, methought, the air grew denser, perfumed from
   an unseen censer
Swung by Seraphim whose foot-falls tinkled on the
   tufted floor.
"Wretch," I cried, "thy God hath lent thee—by these
   angels he hath sent thee
Respite—respite and nepenthe from thy memories of
   Lenore!
Quaff, oh, quaff this kind nepenthe, and forget this lost
   Lenore!"
      Quoth the Raven, "Nevermore."

XV.

"Prophet!" said I, "thing of evil!—prophet still, if
   bird or devil!—
Whether Tempter sent, or whether tempest tossed thee
   here ashore,
Desolate, yet all undaunted, on this desert land en-
   chanted—
On this home by Horror haunted—tell me truly, I im-
   plore—
Is there—*is* there balm in Gilead?—tell me—tell me,
   I implore!"
      Quoth the Raven, "Nevermore."

XVI.

"Prophet!" said I, "thing of evil!—prophet still, if bird or devil!
By that Heaven that bends above us—by that God we both adore—
Tell this soul with sorrow laden if, within the distant Aidenn,
It shall clasp a sainted maiden whom the angels name Lenore—
Clasp a rare and radiant maiden whom the angels name Lenore?"
    Quoth the Raven, "Nevermore."

XVII.

"Be that word our sign of parting, bird or fiend!" I shrieked, upstarting—
"Get thee back into the tempest and the Night's Plutonian shore!
Leave no black plume as a token of that lie thy soul hath spoken!
Leave my loneliness unbroken!—quit the bust above my door!
Take thy beak from out my heart, and take thy form from off my door!"
    Quoth the Raven, "Nevermore."

XVIII.

And the Raven, never flitting, still is sitting, still is sitting,

On the pallid bust of Pallas, just above my chamber
    door;
And his eyes have all the seeming of a demon's that is
    dreaming,
And the lamp-light o'er him streaming throws his shadow
    on the floor;
And my soul from out that shadow that lies floating on
    the floor
        Shall be lifted—nevermore !

Thomas Aird.

Born 1802.

THE HOLY COTTAGE.

"Come near, my child!" the dying father said.
Life's twilight dews lay heavy on his brow.
How softly o'er him did that daughter bow !
She wiped those dews away, she raised his drooping
    head.

He looked upon her with a long long look,
Thinking of all her winning little ways,
His only gladness from her infant days,
Since God from them away the wife and mother took.

The Holy Cottage.

Oft to the moorland places he his child
Led by the hand, or bore upon his back.
The curlew's nest he shewed her in their tract,
And leveret's dewy play upon the whinny wild.

The while he dug, his coat she quaintly dressed
With flowers, aye peeping forth lest he might see
The unfinished fancy; then how pleased when he,
Much wondering, donned her work, when came his
    hour of rest!

Down sate she by him; and when hail or rain
Crossed that high country with its streaming cloud,
She nestled in his bosom o'er her bowed,
Till through the whitening rack looked out the sun again.

And when his axe was in the echoing wood,
Down its shy depths, looking behind her oft,
She o'er the rotting ferns and fungi soft
Thro' boughs and blinding leaves her bursting way
    pursued.

The dry twig, matted in the spear-like grass,
Where fresh from morning's womb the orbèd dew
Lies cold at noon, cracked as she stepped light through,
Startling the cushat out close by the startled lass.

Her fluttering heart was ready then for fear:
Through the far peeping glades she thought she saw

Forms beckoning, luring her; the while with awe
The air grew dark and dumb, listening for something
    drear.

The ferns were stirred, the leaves were shaken, rain
Fell in big drops, and thunder muttered low;
Back burst the flushed dishevelled girl, and O
How glad was she to hear her father's axe again!

Blithe, sitting in the winter night, he made
Or mended by the fire his garden gear;
She with her mates, their faces glancing clear
From shade to ruddy light, quick flitting round him
    played.

And aye some sly young thing, in rosy joyance,
Looked up between his knees, where she was hid;
Humming he worked till she was found, then chid,
But in a way that just lured back the dear annoyance.

Up grew the virgin in her blooming beauty,
Filling her father's ordered house with grace.
And ever o'er the Word she bowed her face,
Binding her days and nights in one continuous duty.

When Sabbath came, she plucked him mint and thyme
And led him forth, what hour from farms around
By style, and sunny croft, and meadow ground,
The particoloured folk came to the bell's sweet chime.

The Holy Cottage.

The simple people, gathered by the sod
Of the new grave, or by the dial-stone,
Made way, and blessed her as she led him on
With short and tottering steps into the House of God.

And holy was their Sabbath afternoon,
The sunlight falling on that father's head
Through their small western casement, as he read
Much to his child of worlds which he must visit
    soon.

And if, his hand upon the book still laid,
His spectacles upraised upon his brow,
Frail nature slept in him, soft going now
She screened the sunny pane, those dear old eyes to
    shade.

Then sitting in' their garden-plot, they saw
With what delicious clearness the far height
Seemed coming near, and slips of falling light
Lay on green moorland spot and soft illumined shaw.

Turned to the sunny hills where he was nursed,
The old man told his child of bloody times,
Marked by the mossy stone of half-sunk rhymes;
And in those hills he saw her sainted mother first.

"I see thy mother now! I see her stand
Waiting for me, and smiling holy sweet;

The robe of white is flowing to her feet;
And O our good Lord Christ, He holds her by the
    hand!

"Farewell, my orphan lamb! To leave thee thus
Is death to me indeed! Yet fear not thou!
On the good Shepherd I do cast thee now:
'Tis but a little while, and thou shalt come to us.

"O yes! no fear! home to us in the skies
His Everlasting arms will carry thee.
Couldst thou thy mother see, as I do see!
My child!" He said, and died. His daughter
    closed his eyes.

Rev. Charles Wolfe.

Born 1791. Died 1823.

THE BURIAL OF SIR JOHN MOORE.*

Not a drum was heard, not a funeral note,
    As his corse to the rampart we hurried:
Not a soldier discharged his farewell shot
    O'er the grave where our hero we buried.

* Sir John Moore was killed in battle by a cannon-ball, at Corunna, in Spain, in 1809.

The Burial of Sir John Moore.

We buried him darkly at dead of night,
    The sods with our bayonets turning;
By the struggling moonbeam's misty light,
    And the lantern dimly burning.

No useless coffin enclosed his breast,
    Nor in sheet or in shroud we bound him;
But he lay like a warrior taking his rest,
    With his martial cloak around him.

Few and short were the prayers we said,
    And we spoke not a word of sorrow,
But we steadfastly gazed on the face of the dead,
    And we bitterly thought on the morrow.

We thought, as we hollowed his narrow bed,
    And smoothed down his lonely pillow,
That the foe and the stranger would tread o'er his head,
    And we far away on the billow.

Lightly they'll talk of the spirit that's gone,
    And o'er his cold ashes upbraid him;
But little he'll reck, if they let him sleep on
    In the grave where a Briton has laid him.

But half of our heavy task was done,
    When the clock struck the hour for retiring;
And we heard the distant and random gun
    That the foe was sullenly firing.

Slowly and sadly we laid him down,
   From the field of his fame fresh and gory ;
We carved not a line, and we raised not a stone,
   But we left him alone with his glory !

William Cullen Bryant.

Born 1794.

THE DAMSEL OF PERU.

Where olive leaves were twinkling in every wind that blew,
There sat beneath the pleasant shade a damsel of Peru.
Betwixt the slender boughs, as they opened to the air,
Came glimpses of her ivory neck and of her glossy hair ;
And sweetly rang her silver voice, within that shady nook,
As from the shrubby glen is heard the sound of hidden brook.

'Tis a song of love and valour, in the noble Spanish tongue,
That once upon the sunny plains of old Castile was sung ;

The Damsel of Peru.   59

When, from their mountain holds, on the Moorish rout
    below,
Had rushed the Christians like a flood, and swept away
    the foe.
Awhile that melody is still, and then breaks forth anew
A wilder rhyme, a livelier note, of freedom and Peru.

For she has bound the sword to a youthful lover's side,
And sent him to the war the day she should have been
    his bride,
And bade him bear a faithful heart to battle for the
    right,
And held the fountains of her eyes till he was out of
    sight.
Since the parting kiss was given, six weary months are fled,
And yet the foe is in the land, and blood must yet be
    shed.

A white hand parts the branches, a lovely face looks
    forth,
And bright dark eyes gaze steadfastly and sadly towards
    the north.
Thou look'st in vain, sweet maiden, the sharpest sight
    would fail,
To spy a sign of human life abroad in all the vale;
For the noon is coming on, and the sunbeams fiercely
    beat,
And the silent hills and forest-tops seem reeling in the
    heat.

That white hand is withdrawn, that fair sad face is gone,
But the music of that silver voice is flowing sweetly on,
Not as of late, in cheerful tones, but mournfully and
    low,—
A ballad of a tender maid heart-broken long ago,
Of him who died in battle, the youthful and the brave,
And her who died of sorrow, upon his early grave.

But see, along that mountain's slope, a fiery horseman
    ride;
Mark his torn plume, his tarnished belt, the sabre at
    his side.
His spurs are buried rowel deep, he rides with loosened
    rein,
There's blood upon his charger's flank and foam upon
    the mane,
He speeds him toward the olive-grove, along that
    shaded hill,—
God shield the helpless maiden there, if he should
    mean her ill!
And suddenly that song has ceased, and suddenly I
    hear
A shriek sent up amid the shade, a shriek—but not of
    fear.
For tender accents follow, and tenderer pauses speak
The overflow of gladness, when words are all too weak:
"I lay my good sword at thy feet, for now Peru is free,
And I am come to dwell beside the olive grove with
    thee."

Charles Swain.
Born 1803.

THE VOICE OF THE MORNING.

The voice of the morning is calling to childhood,
    From streamlet, and valley, and mountain it calls,
And Mary, the loveliest nymph of the wild wood,
    Is crossing the brook where the mill water falls.
Oh! lovely is Mary, her face like a vision
    Once seen leaves a charm that will ever endure;
From her glance and her smile there beams something
    elysian:
She has but one failing—sweet Mary is poor.

Her bosom is white as the hawthorn, and sweeter,
    Her form light and lovesome, as maiden's should be;
Her foot like a fairy's—yet softer and fleeter—
    Oh! Mary, the morn hath no lily like thee.
But narrow and low hangs the roof of her dwelling,
    Her home it is humble, her birth is obscure;
And though in all beauty and sweetness excelling,
    She wanders neglected—for Mary is poor.

Yet, oh! to her heart mother Nature hath given
    The kindest affections that mortal can know;
She loves every star that sheds radiance in heaven,
    She worships the flowers as God's image below.

Ah! sad 'tis to think that a being resembling
   The fairest in beauty, such lot should endure
But the dews that like tears on the lilies are trembling,
   Are types but of Mary—for Mary is poor.

Sir Walter Scott.

Born 1771. Died 1832.

THE BATTLE OF FLODDEN.*

FROM MARMION.

At length the freshening western blast
Aside the shroud of battle cast;
And, first, the ridge of mingled spears
Above the brightening cloud appears;
And in the smoke the pennons flew,
As in the storm the white sea-mew.
Then marked they, dashing broad and far,
The broken billows of the war,
And pluméd crests of chieftains brave,
Floating like foam upon the wave;

---

* The battle of Flodden was fought between the English, commanded by Earl Surrey, and the Scots, commanded by their King, James the Fourth, in 1513. The Scots were defeated, with the loss of from eight to ten thousand men. The English loss was also very great.

The Battle of Flodden.

But nought distinct they see:
Wide raged the battle on the plain;
Spears shook, and falchions flashed amain;
Fell England's arrow-flight like rain;
Crests rose, and stooped, and rose again,
  Wild and disorderly.
Amid the scene of tumult, high
They saw Lord Marmion's falcon fly:
And stainless Tunstall's banner white,
And Edmund Howard's lion bright,
Still bear them bravely in the fight;
  Although against them come,
Of gallant Gordons many a one,
And many a stubborn Badenoch-man,
And many a rugged Border clan,
  With Huntly, and with Home.
Far on the left, unseen the while,
Stanley broke Lennox and Argyle;
Though there the western mountaineer
Rushed with bare bosom on the spear,
And flung the feeble targe aside,
And with both hands the broadsword plied.
'Twas vain:—But Fortune, on the right,
With fickle smile, cheered Scotland's fight,
Then fell that spotless banner white,
  The Howard's lion fell;
Yet still Lord Marmion's falcon flew
With wavering flight, while fiercer grew
  Around the battle-yell.

The Border slogan rent the sky !
A Home! a Gordon! was the cry:
  Loud were the clanging blows;
Advanced,—forced back,—now low, now high,
  The pennon sunk and rose;
As bends the bark's mast in the gale,
When rent are rigging, shrouds, and sail,
  It wavered 'mid the foes.
  *   *   *   *   *   *
By this, though deep the evening fell,
Still rose the battle's deadly swell,
For still the Scots, around their King,
Unbroken, fought in desperate ring.
Where's now their victor vaward wing,
  Where Huntly, and where Home?—
O, for a blast of that dread horn,
On Fontarabian echoes borne,
  That to King Charles did come,
When Rowland brave, and Olivier,
And every paladin and peer,
  On Roncesvalles died !
Such blasts might warn them, not in vain,
To quit the plunder of the slain,
And turn the doubtful day again,
  While yet on Flodden side,
Afar, the Royal Standard flies,
And round it toils, and bleeds, and dies,
  Our Caledonian pride !
In vain the wish—for far away,

While spoil and havoc mark their way,
Near Sybil's Cross the plunderers stray.—
" O, Lady," cried the Monk, " away !"
    And placed her on her steed,
And led her to the chapel fair,
    Of Tilmouth upon Tweed.
There all the night they spent in prayer,
And at the dawn of morning, there
She met her kinsman, Lord Fitz-Clare.
But as they left the darkening heath,
More desperate grew the strife of death.
The English shafts in volleys hailed,
In headlong charge their horse assailed;
From, flank, and rear, the squadrons sweep
To break the Scottish circle deep,
    That fought around their King.
But yet, though thick the shafts as snow,
Though charging knights like whirlwinds go,
Though bill-men ply the ghastly blow,
    Unbroken was the ring;
The stubborn spear-men still made good
Their dark impenetrable wood,
Each stepping where his comrade stood,
    The instant that he fell.
No thought was there of dastard flight;
Linked in the serried phalanx tight,
Groom fought like noble, squire like knight,
    As fearlessly and well;
Till utter darkness closed her wing

O'er their thin host and wounded King.
Then skilful Surrey's sage commands
Led back from strife his shattered bands;
And from the charge they drew,
As mountain-waves, from wasted lands,
    Sweep back to ocean blue.
Then did their loss his foemen know;
Their King, their Lords, their mightiest low,
They melted from the field as snow,
When streams are swoln and south winds blow,
    Dissolves in silent dew.
Tweed's echoes heard the ceaseless plash,
    While many a broken band,
Disordered, through her currents dash;
    To gain the Scottish land;
To town and tower, to down and dale,
To tell red Flodden's dismal tale,
And raise the universal wail.
Tradition, legend, tune, and song,
Shall many an age that wail prolong:
Still from the sire the son shall hear
Of the stern strife, and carnage drear,
    Of Flodden's fatal field,
Where shivered was fair Scotland's spear,
    And broken was her shield!
Day dawns upon the mountain's side:—
There, Scotland! lay thy bravest pride,
Chiefs, knights, and nobles, many a one:
The sad survivors all are gone.—

View not that corpse mistrustfully,
Defaced and mangled though it be;
Nor to yon Border castle high,
Look northward with upbraiding eye;
  Nor cherish hope in vain,
That, journeying far on foreign strand,
The Royal Pilgrim to his land
  May yet return again.
He saw the reck his rashness wrought;
Reckless of life, he desperate fought,
  And fell on Flodden plain:
And well in death his trusty brand,
Firm clenched within his manly hand,
  Beseemed the monarch slain.

Thomas Campbell.

Born 1777. Died 1844.

HOHENLINDEN.*

On Linden when the sun was low,
All bloodless lay the untrodden snow,
And dark as winter was the flow
  Of Iser, rolling rapidly.

* The battle of Hohenlinden, between the French and Austrians, was fought near Munich in 1800.

But Linden saw another sight,
When the drum beat, at dead of night,
Commanding fires of death to light
The darkness of her scenery.

By torch and trumpet fast arrayed,
Each horseman drew his battle-blade,
And furious every charger neighed,
To join the dreadful revelry.

Then shook the hills with thunder riven,
Then rushed the steed to battle driven,
And louder than the bolts of heaven,
Far flashed the red artillery.

But redder yet that light shall glow
On Linden's hills of stainèd snow,
And bloodier yet the torrent flow
Of Iser, rolling rapidly.

'Tis morn, but scarce yon level sun
Can pierce the war-clouds, rolling dun,
Where furious Frank, and fiery Hun,
Shout in their sulph'rous canopy.

The combat deepens. On, ye brave,
Who rush to glory, or the grave!
Wave, Munich! all thy banners wave,
And charge with all thy chivalry!

Few, few, shall part where many meet!
The snow shall be their winding-sheet,
And every turf beneath their feet
Shall be a soldier's sepulchre.

Oliver Goldsmith.

Born 1731. Died 1774.

FROM THE DESERTED VILLAGE.

Sweet Auburn! loveliest village of the plain,
Where health and plenty cheered the labouring swain,
Where smiling spring its earliest visit paid,
And parting summer's lingering blooms delayed
Dear lovely bowers of innocence and ease,
Seats of my youth, when every sport could please,
How often have I loitered o'er thy green,
Where humble happiness endeared each scene!
How often have I paused on every charm,
The sheltered cot, the cultivated farm,
The never-failing brook, the busy mill,
The decent church that topt the neighbouring hill,
The hawthorn bush, with seats beneath the shade,
For talking age and whispering lovers made!
How often have I blest the coming day,
When toil remitting lent its turn to play,

And all the village train, from labour free,
Led up their sports beneath the spreading tree;
While many a pastime circled in the shade,
The young contending as the old surveyed;
And many a gambol frolicked o'er the ground,
And sleights of art and feats of strength went round;
And still as each repeated pleasure tired,
Succeeding sports the mirthful band inspired;
The dancing pair that simply sought renown,
By holding out to tire each other down;
The swain, mistrustless of his smutted face,
While secret laughter tittered round the place;
The bashful virgin's sidelong looks of love,
The matron's glance that would those looks reprove.
These were thy charms, sweet village! sports like these,
With sweet succession, taught even toil to please;
These round thy bowers their cheerful influence shed,
These were thy charms—but all these charms are fled.

Sweet smiling village, loveliest of the lawn,
Thy sports are fled, and all thy charms withdrawn;
Amidst thy bowers the tyrant's hand is seen,
And desolation saddens all thy green:
One only master grasps the whole domain,
And half a tillage stints thy smiling plain;
No more thy glassy brook reflects the day,
But, choked with sedges, works its weedy way;
Along thy glades, a solitary guest,
The hollow-sounding bittern guards its nest;

Amidst thy desert walks the lapwing flies,
And tires their echoes with unvaried cries.
Sunk are thy bowers in shapeless ruin all,
And the long grass o'ertops the mouldering wall;
And, trembling, shrinking from the spoiler's hand,
Far, far away, thy children leave the land.

Ill fares the land, to hastening ills a prey,
Where wealth accumulates, and men decay:
Princes and lords may flourish, or may fade;
A breath can make them as a breath has made;
But a bold peasantry, their country's pride,
When once destroyed, can never be supplied.

A time there was, ere England's griefs began,
When every rood of ground maintained its man;
For him light labour spread her wholesome store,
Just gave what life required, but gave no more:
His best companions, innocence and health,
And his best riches, ignorance of wealth.

But times are altered; trade's unfeeling train
Usurp the land, and dispossess the swain:
Along the lawn where scattered hamlets rose,
Unwieldy wealth and cumbrous pomp repose;
And every want to opulence allied,
And every pang that folly pays to pride.
Those gentle hours that plenty bade to bloom,
Those calm desires that asked but little room,

Those healthful sports that graced the peaceful scene,
Lived in each look, and brightened all the green;
These, far departing, seek a kinder shore,
And rural mirth and manners are no more.

Sweet Auburn! parent of the blissful hour,
Thy glades forlorn confess the tyrant's power.
Here, as I take my solitary rounds,
Amidst thy tangling walks, and ruined grounds,
And, many a year elapsed, return to view
Where once the cottage stood, the hawthorn grew,
Remembrance wakes, with all her busy train,
Swells at my breast, and turns the past to pain.

In all my wanderings round this world of care,
In all my griefs—and God has given my share—
I still had hopes my latest hours to crown,
Amidst these humble bowers to lay me down;
To husband out life's taper at the close,
And keep the flame from wasting by repose:
I still had hopes, for pride attends us still,
Amidst the swains to shew my book-learned skill,
Around my fire an evening group to draw,
And tell of all I felt, and all I saw;
And, as a hare whom hounds and horns pursue,
Pants to the place from whence at first he flew,
I still had hopes, my long vexations past,
Here to return—and die at home at last.

William Collins.

Born 1720. Died 1756.

THE PASSIONS.

When Music, heavenly maid, was young,
While yet in early Greece she sung,
The Passions oft, to hear her shell,
Thronged around her magic cell,
Exulting, trembling, raging, fainting,
Possest beyond the muse's painting ;
By turns they felt the glowing mind
Disturbed, delighted, raised, refined.
Till once, 'tis said, when all were fired,
Filled with fury, rapt, inspired,
From the supporting myrtles round
They snatched her instruments of sound,
And as they oft had heard apart
Sweet lessons of her forceful art,
Each, for madness ruled the hour,
Would prove his own expressive power.

First Fear his hand, its skill to try,
   Amid the chords bewildered laid,
And back recoiled, he knew not why,
   Even at the sound himself had made.

Next Anger rushed, his eyes on fire,
  In lightnings owned his secret stings,
In one rude clash he struck the lyre,
  And swept with hurried hand the strings.

With woeful measures wan Despair—
  Low sullen sounds his grief beguiled,
A solemn, strange, and mingled air,
  'T was sad by fits, by starts 'twas wild.

But thou, O Hope, with eyes so fair,
  What was thy delighted measure?
Still it whispered promised Pleasure,
  And bade the lovely scenes at distance hail!
Still would her touch the strain prolong,
  And from the rocks, the woods, the vale,
She called on Echo still through all the song;
  And where her sweetest theme she chose,
  A soft responsive voice was heard at every close,
And Hope inchanted, smiled, and waved her
    golden hair.
And longer had she sung—but, with a frown,
  Revenge impatient rose,
He threw his blood-stained sword in thunder down.
    And, with a withering look,
    The war-denouncing trumpet took,
And blew a blast so loud and dread,
Were ne'er prophetic sounds so full of woe.
  And ever and anon he beat

The Passions.

The doubling drum with furious heat;
And though sometimes, each dreary pause between,
   Dejected Pity at his side
   Her soul-subduing voice applied,
Yet still he kept his wild unaltered mien,
While each strained ball of sight seemed bursting from his head.
Thy numbers, jealousy, to nought were fixed,
   Sad proof of thy distressful state,
Of differing themes the veering song was mixed,
   And now it courted Love, now raving called on Hate.
With eyes upraised, as one inspired,
Pale Melancholy sat retired,
And from her wild sequestered seat,
In notes by distance made more sweet,
Poured through the mellow horn her pensive soul;
   And dashing soft from rocks around,
   Bubbling runnels joined the sound;
Through glades and glooms the mingled measure stole
   Or o'er some haunted streams with fond delay,
     Round an holy calm diffusing,
     Love of peace and lonely musing,
   In hollow murmurs died away.
But, O, how altered was its sprightlier tone!
When Cheerfulness, a nymph of healthiest hue!
   Her bow across her shoulder flung,
   Her buskins gemmed with morning dew,
Blew an inspiring air, that dale and thicket rung,

The hunter's call to Faun and Dryad known;
The oak-crowned sisters, and their chaste-eyed queen,
Satyrs and sylvan boys were seen,
Peeping from forth their alleys green;
Brown Exercise rejoiced to hear,
And Sport leapt up, and seized his beechen spear.
Last came Joy's ecstatic trial,
He, with viney crown advancing,
First to the lively pipe his hand addrest,
But soon he saw the brisk-awakening viol,
Whose sweet entrancing voice he loved the best.
They would have thought, who heard the strain,
They saw in Tempe's vale her native maids,
Amidst the festal sounding shades,
To some unwearied minstrel dancing,
While, as his flying fingers kissed the strings,
Love framed with Mirth a gay fantastic round,
Loose were her tresses seen, her zone unbound,
And he, amidst his frolic play,
As if he would the charming air repay,
Shook thousand odours from his dewy wings.
O Music, sphere-descended maid,
Friend of pleasure, wisdom's aid,
Why, goddess, why to us denied?
Layest thou thy ancient lyre aside?
As in that loved Athenian bower,
You learned in all-commanding power,
Thy mimic soul, O nymph endeared,
Can well recall what then it heard.

Where is thy native simple heart,
Devote to Virtue, Fancy, Art?
Arise, as in that elder time,
Warm, energic, chaste, sublime!
Thy wonders, in that godlike age,
Fill thy recording sister's page—
'Tis said, and I believe the tale,
Thy humblest reed could more prevail,
Had more of strength, diviner rage,
Than all which charms this laggard age,
Even all at once together found
Cecilia's mingled world of sound—
O, bid our vain endeavours cease,
Revive the just designs of Greece,
Return in all thy simple state!
Confirm the tales her sons relate!

Thomas Gray.

Born 1716. Died 1771.

ELEGY WRITTEN IN A COUNTRY CHURCH-YARD.

The Curfew tolls the knell of parting day,
The lowing herd wind slowly o'er the lea,
The ploughman homeward plods his weary way,
And leaves the world to darkness and to me.

Now fades the glimmering landscape on the sight,
And all the air a solemn stillness holds,
Save where the beetle wheels his droning flight,
And drowsy tinklings lull the distant folds;
Save that from yonder ivy-mantled tower,
The moping owl does to the moon complain
Of such, as wandering near her secret bower,
Molest her ancient solitary reign.
Beneath those rugged elms, that yew-tree's shade,
Where heaves the turf in many a mouldering heap,
Each in his narrow cell for ever laid,
The rude Forefathers of the hamlet sleep.
The breezy call of incense-breathing Morn,
The swallow twittering from the straw-built shed,
The cock's shrill clarion, or the echoing horn,
No more shall rouse them from their lowly bed.
For them no more the blazing hearth shall burn,
Or busy housewife ply her evening care:
No children run to lisp their sire's return,
Or climb his knees the envied kiss to share.
Oft did the harvest to their sickle yield,
Their furrow oft the stubborn glebe has broke;
How jocund did they drive their team afield!
How bowed the woods beneath their sturdy stroke!
Let not Ambition mock their useful toil,
Their homely joys, and destiny obscure;
Nor Grandeur hear with a disdainful smile,
The short and simple annals of the poor.
The boast of heraldry, the pomp of power,

And all that beauty, all that wealth e'er gave,
Await alike the inevitable hour.
The paths of glory lead but to the grave.
Nor you, ye proud, impute to these the fault,
If Memory o'er their tomb no trophies raise,
Where through the long-drawn isle and fretted vault
The pealing anthem swells the note of praise.
Can storied urn or animated bust
Back to its mansion call the fleeting breath?
Can Honour's voice provoke the silent dust,
Or Flattery sooth the dull cold ear of Death?
Perhaps in this neglected spot is laid
Some heart once pregnant with celestial fire;
Hands, that the rod of empire might have swayed,
Or waked to ecstasy the living lyre.
But Knowledge to their eyes her ample page
Rich with the spoils of time did ne'er unroll;
Chill Penury repressed their noble rage,
And froze the genial current of the soul.
Full many a gem of purest ray serene,
The dark unfathomed caves of ocean bear:
Full many a flower is born to blush unseen,
And waste its sweetness on the desert air.
Some village-Hampden, that with dauntless breast
The little Tyrant of his fields withstood;
Some mute inglorious Milton here may rest,
Some Cromwell guiltless of his country's blood.
The applause of listening senates to command,
The threats of pain and ruin to despise,

To scatter plenty o'er a smiling land,
And read their hist'ry in a nation's eyes,
Their lot forbad: nor circumscribed alone
Their growing virtues, but their crimes confined;
Forbad to wade through slaughter to a throne,
And shut the gates of mercy on mankind,
The struggling pangs of conscious truth to hide,
To quench the blushes of ingenuous shame,
Or heap the shrine of Luxury and Pride
With incense kindled at the Muse's flame.
Far from the madding crowd's ignoble strife,
Their sober wishes never learned to stray;
Along the cool sequestered vale of life
They kept the noiseless tenor of their way.
Yet even these bones from insult to protect
Some frail memorial still erected nigh,
With uncouth rhymes and shapeless sculpture decked,
Implores the passing tribute of a sigh.
Their names, their years, spelt by the unlettered muse,
The place of fame and elegy supply;
And many a holy text around she strews,
That teach the rustic moralist to die.
For who to dumb forgetfulness a prey,
This pleasing anxious being e'er resigned,
Left the warm precincts of the cheerful day,
Nor cast one longing lingering look behind?
On some fond breast the parting soul relies,
Some pious drops the closing eye requires;
Even from the tomb the voice of nature cries,

Even in our ashes live their wonted fires.
For thee, who mindful of the unhonoured dead
Dost in these lines their artless tale relate ;
If chance, by lonely contemplation led,
Some kindred spirit shall inquire thy fate,
Haply some hoary-headed swain may say,
"Oft have we seen him at the peep of dawn
Brushing with hasty steps the dews away
To meet the sun upon the upland lawn.
There at the foot of yonder nodding beech
That wreathes its old fantastic roots so high,
His listless length at noontide would be stretch,
And pore upon the brook that babbles by.
Hard by yon wood, now smiling as in scorn,
Muttering his wayward fancies he would rove ;
Now drooping, woeful wan, like one forlorn,
Or crazed with care, or crossed in hopeless love.
One morn I missed him on the customed hill,
Along the heath and near his favourite tree ;
Another came ; nor yet beside the rill,
Nor up the lawn, nor at the wood was he ;
The next with dirges due in sad array
Slow through the church-way path we saw him borne.
Approach and read (for thou canst read) the lay,
Graved on the stone beneath yon aged thorn."

THE EPITAPH.

Here rests his head upon the lap of earth,
A youth to fortune and to fame unknown;
Fair science frowned not on his humble birth,
And melancholy marked him for her own.
Large was his bounty, and his soul sincere,
Heaven did a recompense as largely send:
He gave to misery all he had, a tear,
He gained from Heaven ('twas all he wished) a friend.
No farther seek his merits to disclose,
Or draw his frailties from their dread abode,
(There they alike in trembling hope repose),
The bosom of his Father and his God.

Henry Kirke White.

Born 1785.   Died 1806.

FROM CLIFTON GROVE.

Lo! in the west, fast fades the lingering light,
And day's last vestige takes its silent flight.
No more is heard the woodman's measured stroke
Which, with the dawn, from yonder dingle broke;
No more, hoarse clamouring o'er the uplifted head,
The crows assembling, seek their wind-rocked bed.

Stilled is the village hum—the woodland sounds
Have ceased to echo o'er the dewy grounds,
And general silence reigns, save when below,
The murmuring Trent is scarcely heard to flow;
And save when, swung by 'nighted rustic late,
Oft, on its hinge, rebounds the jarring gate:
Or, when the sheep bell, in the distant vale,
Breathes its wild music on the downy gale.

Now, when the rustic wears the social smile,
Released from day and its attendant toil,
And draws his household round their evening fire,
And tells the oft-told tales that never tire:
Or, where the town's blue turrets dimly rise,
And manufacture taints the ambient skies,
The pale mechanic leaves the labouring loom,
The air-pent hold, the pestilential room,
And rushes out, impatient to begin
The stated course of customary sin:
Now, now, my solitary way I bend
Where solemn groves in awful state impend,
And cliffs, that boldly rise above the plain,
Bespeak, blest Clifton! thy sublime domain.
Here, lonely wandering o'er the sylvan bower,
I come to pass the meditative hour;
To bid awhile the strife of passion cease,
And woo the calms of solitude and peace.
And oh! thou sacred power, who rear'st on high
Thy leafy throne where waving poplars sigh!

Genius of woodland shades! whose mild control
Steals with resistless witchery to the soul,
Come with thy wonted ardour and inspire
My glowing bosom with thy hallowed fire.
And thou, too, Fancy! from thy starry sphere,
Where to the hymning orbs thou lend'st thine ear,
Do thou descend, and bless my ravished sight,
Veiled in soft visions of serene delight.
At thy command the gale that passes by
Bears in its whispers mystic harmony.
Thou wavest thy wand, and lo! what forms appear!
On the dark cloud what giant shapes career!
The ghosts of Ossian skim the misty vale,
And hosts of sylphids on the moon-beam sail.

This gloomy alcove, darkling to the sight,
Where meeting trees create eternal night;
Save, when from yonder stream, the sunny ray,
Reflected gives a dubious gleam of day;
Recalls endearing to my altered mind,
Times, when beneath the boxen hedge reclined
I watched the lapwing to her clamorous brood;
Or lured the robin to its scattered food;
Or woke with song the woodland echo wild,
And at each gay response delighted, smiled.
How oft, when childhood threw its golden ray
Of gay romance o'er every happy day,
Here would I run, a visionary boy,
When the hoarse tempest shook the vaulted sky,

And fancy-led, beheld the Almighty's form
Sternly careering on the eddying storm;
And heard, while awe congealed my inmost soul,
His voice terrific in the thunders roll.
With secret joy, I viewed with vivid glare,
The volleyed lightnings cleave the sullen air;
And, as the warring winds around reviled,
With awful pleasure big,—I heard and smiled.
Beloved remembrance!—Memory which endears
This silent spot to my advancing years.
Here dwells eternal peace, eternal rest,
In shades like these to live, is to be blest.
While happiness evades the busy crowd,
In rural coverts loves the maid to shroud.
And thou, too, Inspiration, whose wild flame
Shoots with electric swiftness through the frame,
Thou here dost love to sit, with up-turned eye,
And listen to the stream that murmurs by,
The woods that wave, the gray-owl's silken flight,
The mellow music of the listening night.
Congenial calms more welcome to my breast
Than maddening joy in dazzling lustre drest,
To heaven my prayers, my daily prayers I raise,
That ye may bless my unambitious days,
Withdrawn, remote, from all the haunts of strife
May trace with me the lowly vale of life,
And when her banner Death shall o'er me wave.
May keep your peaceful vigils on my grave.
Now, as I rove, where wide the prospect grows,

A livelier light upon my vision flows.
No more above, the embracing branches meet;
No' more the river gurgles at my feet,
But seen deep down the cliff's impending side
Through hanging woods, now gleams its silver tide.
Dim is my upland path,—across the Green
Fantastic shadows fling, yet oft between
The chequered glooms, the moon her chaste ray sheds,
Where knots of blue-bells droop their graceful heads,
And beds of violets blooming 'mid the trees,
Load with waste fragrance the nocturnal breeze.

Say, why does man, while to his opening sight,
Each shrub presents a source of chaste delight,
And Nature bids for him her treasures flow,
And gives to him alone, his bliss to know,
Why does he pant for Vice's deadly charms?
Why clasp the syren Pleasure to his arms?
And suck deep draughts of her voluptuous breath,
Though fraught with ruin, infamy, and death?
Could he who thus to vile enjoyments clings,
Know what calm joy from purer sources springs,
Could he but feel how sweet, how free from strife,
The harmless pleasures of a harmless life,
No more his soul would pant for joys impure,
The deadly chalice would no more allure,
But the sweet portion he was wont to sip,
Would turn to poison on his conscious lip.

Samuel Taylor Coleridge.

Born 1772. Died 1834.

LOVE.

All thoughts, all passions, all delights,
Whatever stirs this mortal frame,
All are but ministers of Love,
    And feed his sacred flame.

Oft in my waking dreams do I
Live o'er again that happy hour,
When midway on the mount I lay,
    Beside the ruined tower.

The moonshine, stealing o'er the scene
Had blended with the lights of eve;
And she was there, my hope, my joy,
    My own dear Genevieve!

She leaned against the armèd man,
The statue of the armèd knight;
She stood and listened to my lay,
    Amid the lingering light.

Few sorrows hath she of her own.
My hope! my joy! my Genevieve;

She loves me best whene'er I sing
    The songs that make her grieve.

I played a soft and doleful air,
I sang an old and moving story—
An old rude song, that suited well
    That ruin wild and hoary.

She listened with a flitting blush,
With downcast eyes and modest grace;
For well she knew I could not choose
    But gaze upon her face.

I told her of the Knight that wore
Upon his shield a burning brand;
And that for ten long years he wooed
    The Lady of the Land.

I told her how he pined: and ah!
The deep, the low, the pleading tone
With which I sang another's love,
    Interpreted my own.

She listened with a flitting blush,
With downcast eyes, and modest grace;
And she forgave me, that I gazed
    Too fondly on her face!

But when I told the cruel scorn

That crazed that bold and lovely Knight,
And that he crossed the mountain-woods,
   Nor rested day nor night ;

That sometimes from the savage den,
And sometimes from the darksome shade,
And sometimes starting up at once
   In green and sunny glade,—

There came and looked him in the face
An angel beautiful and bright ;
And that he knew it was a Fiend,
   This miserable Knight !

And that unknowing what he did,
He leaped amid a murderous band,
And saved from outrage worse than death
   The Lady of the Land ;—

And how she wept, and clasped his knees ;
And how she tended him in vain—
And ever strove to expiate
   The scorn that crazed his brain ;—

And that she nursed him in a cave ;
And how his madness went away,
When on the yellow forest-leaves
   A dying man he lay ;—

Samuel Taylor Coleridge.

His dying words—but when I reached
That tenderest strain of all the ditty,
My faltering voice and pausing harp
    Disturbed her soul with pity!

All impulses of soul and sense
Had thrilled my guileless Genevieve;
The music and the doleful tale,
    The rich and balmy eve;

And hopes, and fears that kindle hope,
An undistinguishable throng,
And gentle wishes long subdued,
    Subdued and cherished long!

She wept with pity and delight,
She blushed with love, and virgin shame;
And like the murmur of a dream,
    I heard her breathe my name.

Her bosom heaved—she stepped aside,
As conscious of my look she stept—
Then suddenly, with timorous eye
    She fled to me and wept.

She half inclosed me with her arms,
She pressed me with a meek embrace;
And bending back her head, looked up,
    And gazed upon my face.

'Twas partly love, and partly fear,
And partly 'twas a bashful art,
That I might rather feel, than see,
   The swelling of her heart.

I calmed her fears, and she was calm,
And told her love with virgin pride;
And so I won my Genevieve,
   My bright and beauteous Bride.

Robert Bloomfield.

Born 1766. Died 1823.

SONG FOR A HIGHLAND DROVER RETURNING FROM ENGLAND.

Now fare-thee-well, England: no further I'll roam;
But follow my shadow that points the way home:
Your gay southern shores shall not tempt me to stay;
For my Maggy's at home, and my children at play!
'Tis this makes my bonnet sit light on my brow,
Gives my sinews their strength and my bosom its glow.

Farewell, mountaineers! my companions, adieu;
Soon, many long miles when I'm severed from you,

I shall miss your white horns on the brink of the burn,
And o'er the rough heaths, where you'll never return;
But in brave English pastures you cannot complain,
While your drover speeds back to his Maggy again.

O Tweed! gentle Tweed, as I pass your green vales,
More than life, more than love, my tired spirit inhales;
There Scotland, my darling, lies full in my view,
With her bare-footed lasses and mountains so blue;
To the mountains away; my heart bounds like the hind
For home is so sweet, and my Maggy so kind.

As day after day I still follow my course,
And in fancy trace back every stream to its source,
Hope cheers me up hills, where the road lies before,
O'er hills just as high, and o'er tracks of wild moor;
The keen polar star nightly rising to view;
But Maggy's my star, just as steady and true.

O ghosts of my fathers! O heroes, look down!
Fix my wandering thoughts on your deeds of renown;
For the glory of Scotland reigns warm in my breast,
And fortitude grows both from toil and from rest;
May your deeds and your worth be for ever in view,
And may Maggy bear sons not unworthy of you.

Love, why do you urge me, so weary and poor?
I cannot step faster, I cannot do more:
I've passed silver Tweed; e'en the Tay flows behind:

Yet fatigue I'll disdain;—my reward I shall find;
Thou, sweet smile of innocence, thou art my prize;
And the joy that will sparkle in Maggy's blue eyes.

She'll watch to the southward;—perhaps she will sigh,
That the way is so long, and the mountains so high;
Perhaps some huge rock in the dusk she may see,
And will say in her fondness, "that surely is he!"
Good wife, you're deceived; I'm still far from my home;
Go, sleep, my dear Maggy,—to-morrow I'll come.

Rev. Edward Young.

Born 1681. Died 1765.

FROM THE LAST DAY.

The fatal period, the great hour, is come,
And nature shrinks at her approaching doom;
Loud peals of thunder give the sign, and all
Heaven's terrors in array surround the ball;
Sharp lightnings with the meteor's blaze conspire,
And, darted downward, set the world on fire;
Black rising clouds the thickened ether choke,
And spiry flames dart through the rolling smoke,
With keen vibrations cut the sullen night,

And strike the darkened sky with dreadful light;
From heaven's four regions, with immortal force,
Angels drive on the wind's impetuous course,
T' enrage the flame: it spreads, it soars on high,
Swells in the storm, and billows through the sky:
Here winding pyramids of fire ascend,
Cities and deserts in one ruin blend;
Here blazing volumes wafted, overwhelm
The spacious face of a far-distant realm;
There, undermined, down rush eternal hills,
The neighbouring vales the vast destruction fills.
Hear'st thou that dreadful crack? that sound which broke
Like peals of thunder, and the centre shook?
What wonders must that groan of nature tell!
Olympus there, and mightier Atlas, fell;
Which seemed above the reach of fate to stand,
A towering monument of God's right hand;
Now dust and smoke, whose brow so lately spread
O'er sheltered countries its diffusive shade.

 Shew me that celebrated spot, where all
The various rulers of the severed ball
Have humbly sought wealth, honour, and redress,
That land which heaven seemed diligent to bless,
Once called Britannia: Can her glories end?
And can't surrounding seas her realms defend?
Alas! in flames behold surrounding seas!
Like oil, their waters but augment the blaze.

 Some angel, say where ran proud Asia's bound?
Or where with fruits was fair Europa crowned?

Where stretched waste Libya? Where did India's store
Sparkle in diamonds, and her golden ore?
Each lost in each, their mingling kingdoms glow,
And all dissolved, one fiery deluge flow:
Thus earth's contending monarchies are joined,
And a full period of ambition find.
 And now whate'er or swims, or walks, or flies,
Inhabitants of sea, or earth, or skies;
All on whom Adam's wisdom fixed a name,
All plunge, and perish in the conquering flame.

Thomas Moore.

Born 1779. Died 1852.

FROM LALLA ROOKH.

Fly to the desert, fly with me,
Our Arab tents are rude for thee;
But, oh! the choice what heart can doubt,
Of tents with love, or thrones without?

Our rocks are rough, but smiling there
The acacia waves her yellow hair,
Lonely and sweet, nor loved the less
For flowering in a wilderness.

Our sands are bare, but down their slope
The silvery-footed antelope
As gracefully and gaily springs
As o'er the marble courts of kings.

Then come—thy Arab maid will be
The loved and lone acacia-tree,
The antelope, whose feet shall bless
With their light sound thy loneliness.

Oh! there are looks and tones that dart
An instant sunshine through the heart,—
As if the soul that minute caught
Some treasure it through life had sought;

As if the very lips and eyes,
Predestined to have all our sighs,
And never be forgot again,
Sparkled and spoke before us then!

So came thy every glance and tone
When first on me they breathed and shone;
New, as if brought from other spheres,
Yet welcome as if loved for years.

Then fly with me,—if thou hast known
No other flame, nor falsely thrown
A gem away, that thou hadst sworn
Should ever in thy heart be worn.

Come, if the love thou hast for me,
Is pure and fresh as mine for thee,—
Fresh as the fountain under ground,
When first 'tis by the lapwing found.*

But if for me thou dost forsake
Some other maid, and rudely break
Her worshipped image from its base,
To give to me the ruined place ;—

Then, fare thee well—I'd rather make
My bower upon some icy lake
When thawing suns begin to shine,
Than trust to love so false as thine !

Robert Southey.

Born 1774.   Died 1843.

THE MISER'S MANSION.

Thou mouldering mansion, whose embattled side
  Shakes as about to fall at every blast ;
Once the gay pile of splendour, wealth, and pride,
  But now the monument of grandeur past.

* The lapwing is fabulously supposed to be gifted with the power of indicating where water is to be found beneath the ground.

Fallen fabric! pondering o'er thy time traced-walls,
    Thy mouldering, mighty, melancholy state;
Each object to the musing mind recalls
    The sad vicissitudes of varying fate.

Thy tall towers tremble to the touch of time,
    The rank weeds rustle in thy spacious courts;
Filled are thy wide canals with loathly slime,
    Where, battening undisturbed, the foul toad sports.

Deep from her dismal dwelling yells the owl,
    The shrill bat flits around her dark retreat;
And the hoarse daw, when loud the tempests howl,
    Screams as the wild winds shake her secret seat.

'Twas here Avaro dwelt, who daily told
    His useless heaps of wealth in selfish joy;
Who loved to ruminate o'er hoarded gold,
    And hid those stores he dreaded to employ.

In vain to him benignant heaven bestowed
    The golden heaps to render thousands blest;
Smooth agèd penury's laborious road,
    And heal the sorrows of affliction's breast.

For, like the serpent of romance, he lay
    Sleepless and stern to guard the golden sight;
With ceaseless care he watched his heaps by day,
    With causeless fears he agonized by night.

The Miser's Mansion.

Ye honest rustics, whose diurnal toil
   Enriched the ample fields this churl possest;
Say, ye who paid to him the annual spoil,
   With all his riches, was Avaro blest?

Rose he, like you, at morn, devoid of fear,
   His anxious vigils o'er his gold to keep?
Or sunk he, when the noiseless night was near,
   As calmly on his couch of down to sleep?

Thou wretch! thus curst with poverty of soul,
   What boot to thee the blessings fortune gave?
What boots thy wealth above the world's control,
   If riches doom their churlish lord a slave?

Chilled at thy presence grew the stately halls,
   Nor longer echoed to the song of mirth;
The hand of art no more adorned thy walls,
   Nor blazed with hospitable fires the hearth.

On well-worn hinges turns the gate no more,
   Nor social friendship hastes the friend to meet;
Nor, when the accustomed guest draws near the door,
   Run the glad dogs, and gambol round his feet.

Sullen and stern Avaro sat alone,
   In anxious wealth amid the joyless hall,
Nor heeds the chilly hearth with moss o'ergrown,
   Nor sees the green slime mark the mouldering wall.

For desolation o'er the fabric dwells,
   And time, on restless pinion, hurried by;
Loud from her chimney'd seat the night-bird yells,
   And through the shattered roof descends the sky.

Thou melancholy mansion! much mine eye
   Delights to wander o'er thy sullen gloom,
And mark the daw from yonder turret fly,
   And muse how man himself creates his doom.

For here, had justice reigned, had pity known
   With genial power to sway Avaro's breast,
These treasured heaps which fortune made his own,
   By aiding misery might himself have blest.

And charity had oped her golden store,
   To work the gracious will of heaven intent,
Fed from her superflux the craving poor,
   And paid adversity what heaven had lent.

Then had thy turrets stood in all their state,
   Then had the hand of art adorned thy wall,
Swift on its well-worn hinges turned the gate,
   And friendly converse cheered the echoing hall.

Then had the village youth at vernal hour
   Hung round with flowery wreaths thy friendly gate,
And blest in gratitude that sovereign power
   That made the man of mercy good as great.

The traveller then to view thy towers had stood,
  Whilst babes had lisped their benefactor's name,
And called on Heaven to give thee every good,
  And told abroad thy hospitable fame.

In every joy of life the hours had fled,
  Whilst time on downy pinions hurried by,
'Till age with silver hairs had graced thy head,
  Weaned from the world, and taught thee how to die.

And, as thy liberal hand had showered around
  The ample wealth by lavish fortune given,
Thy parted spirit had that justice found,
  And angels hymned the rich man's soul to heaven.

William Wordsworth.

Born 1770. Died 1850.

YARROW VISITED.

And is this Yarrow?—*this* the stream
Of which my fancy cherished,
So faithfully, a waking dream?
An image that hath perished!
O that some minstrel's harp were near,
To utter notes of gladness,

And chase this silence from the air,
That fills my heart with sadness!

Yet why?—a silvery current flows
With uncontrolled meanderings;
Nor have these eyes by greener hills
Been soothed, in all my wanderings.
And, through her depths, Saint Mary's Lake
Is visibly delighted;
For not a feature of those hills
Is in the mirror slighted.

A blue sky bends o'er Yarrow Vale,
Save where that pearly whiteness
Is round the rising sun diffused,
A tender hazy brightness;
Mild dawn of promise! that excludes
All profitless dejection;
Though not unwilling here t' admit
A pensive recollection.

Where was it that the famous flower
Of Yarrow Vale lay bleeding?
His bed perchance was yon smooth mound
On which the herd is feeding:
And haply from this crystal pool,
Now peaceful as the morning,
The water-wraith ascended thrice,
And gave his doleful warning.

Delicious is the lay that sings
The haunts of happy lovers,
The path that leads them to the grove,
The leafy grove that covers:
And pity sanctifies the verse
That paints, by strength of sorrow,
The unconquerable strength of love;
Bear witness, rueful Yarrow!

But thou, that didst appear so fair
To fond imagination,
Dost rival in the light of day
Her delicate creation:
Meek loveliness is round thee spread,
A softness still and holy;
The grace of forest charms decayed,
And pastoral melancholy.

That region left, the vale unfolds
Rich groves of lofty stature,
With Yarrow winding through the pomp
Of cultivated nature;
And, rising from those lofty groves,
Behold a ruin hoary!
The shattered front of Newark's towers,
Renowned in border story.

Fair scenes for childhood's opening bloom,
For sportive youth to stray in;

For manhood to enjoy his strength;
And age to wear away in!
Yon cottage seems a bower of bliss,
It promises protection
To studious ease, and generous cares,
And every chaste affection!

How sweet on this autumnal day,
The wild wood's fruits to gather,
And on my true love's forehead plant
A crest of blooming heather!
And what if I enwreathed my own!
'Twere no offence to reason;
The sober hills thus deck their brows
To meet the wintry season.

I see—but not by sight alone,
Loved Yarrow, have I won thee;
A ray of fancy still survives—
Her sunshine plays upon thee!
Thy ever youthful waters keep
A course of lively pleasure;
And gladsome notes my lips can breathe,
Accordant to the measure.

The vapours linger round the heights,
They melt—and soon must vanish;
One hour is theirs, nor more is mine—
Sad thought! which I would banish,

But that I know, where'er I go,
Thy genuine image, Yarrow!
Will dwell with me—to heighten joy,
And cheer my mind in sorrow.

James Montgomery.

Born 1771. Died 1854.

A MOTHER'S LOVE.

A MOTHER'S LOVE,—how sweet the name!
  What *is* a Mother's love?
—A noble, pure, and tender flame,
  Enkindled from above,
To bless a heart of earthly mould;
The warmest love that *can* grow cold;
  This is a Mother's Love.

To bring a helpless babe to light,
  Then, while it lies forlorn,
To gaze upon that dearest sight,
  And feel herself new-born,
In its existence lose her own,
And live and breathe in it alone;
  This is a Mother's Love.

Its weakness in her arms to bear ;
  To cherish on her breast,
Feed it from Love's own fountain there,
  And lull it there to rest ;
Then, while it slumbers, watch its breath,
As if to guard from instant death ;
  This is a Mother's Love.

To mark its growth from day to day,
  Its opening charms admire,
Catch from its eye the earliest ray
  Of intellectual fire ;
To smile and listen while it talks,
And lend a finger when it walks ;
  This is a Mother's Love.

And can a Mother's Love grow cold ?
  Can she forget her boy ?
His pleading innocence behold,
  Nor weep for grief—for joy ?
A Mother may forget her child,
While wolves devour it on the wild ;
  Is *this* a Mother's Love ?

Ten thousand voices answer " No !"
  Ye clasp your babes and kiss ;
Your bosoms yearn, your eyes o'erflow ;
  Yet, ah ! remember this,—
The infant, reared alone for earth,

May live, may die,—to curse his birth;
—Is *this* a Mother's Love?

A parent's heart may prove a snare;
　The child she loves so well,
Her hand may lead, with gentlest care,
　Down the smooth road to hell;
Nourish its frame,—destroy its mind:
Thus do the blind mislead the blind,
　Even with a Mother's Love.

Blest infant! whom his mother taught
　Early to seek the Lord,
And poured upon his dawning thought
　The day-spring of the word;
This was the lesson to her son
—Time is Eternity begun:
　Behold that Mother's Love.

Blest Mother! who, in wisdom's path
　By her own parent trod,
Thus taught her son to flee the wrath,
　And know the fear, of God:
Ah, youth! like him enjoy your prime;
Begin Eternity in time,
　Taught by that Mother's Love.

That Mother's Love!—how sweet the name!
　What *was* that Mother's Love?

—The noblest, purest, tenderest flame,
That kindles from above,
Within a heart of earthly mould,
As much of heaven as heart can hold,
Nor through eternity grows cold:
This was that Mother's Love.

William Shakspere.

Born 1564.   Died 1616.

DIRGE IN CYMBELINE.

FEAR no more the heat o' the sun,
  Nor the furious winter's rages;
Thou thy worldly task hast done,
  Home art gone, and ta'en thy wages:
Golden lads and girls all must,
As chimney-sweepers, come to dust.

Fear no more the frown o' the great,
  Thou art past the tyrant's stroke;
Care no more to clothe, and eat;
  To thee the reed is as the oak:
The sceptre, learning, physick, must
All follow this, and come to dust.

Fear no more the lightning-flash,
Nor the all-dreaded thunder stone;
Fear not slander, censure rash;
Thou hast finished joy and moan:
All lovers young, all lovers must
Consign to thee, and come to dust.

No exorciser harm thee!
Nor no witchcraft charm thee!
Ghost unlaid forbear thee!
Nothing ill come near thee!
Quiet consummation have;
And renownèd be thy grave!

John Milton.

Born 1608. Died 1674.

SATAN'S ADDRESS TO THE SUN

FROM PARADISE LOST.

O THOU that, with surpassing glory crowned,
Lookest from thy sole dominion like the god
Of this new world; at whose sight all the stars
Hide their diminished heads; to thee I call,
But with no friendly voice, and add thy name,

O Sun, to tell thee how I hate thy beams,
That bring to my remembrance from what state
I fell, how glorious once above thy sphere;
Till pride, and worse ambition, threw me down,
Warring in heaven against heaven's matchless King.
Ah wherefore! he deserved no such return
From me, whom he created what I was,
In that bright eminence, and with his good
Upbraided none; nor was his service hard.
What could be less, than to afford him praise,
The easiest recompense, and pay him thanks,
How due! yet all his good proved ill in me,
And wrought but malice; lifted up so high
I sdained subjection, and thought one step higher
Would set me highest, and in a moment quit
The debt immense of endless gratitude,
So burdensome still paying, still to owe,
Forgetful what from him I still received;
And understood not that a grateful mind
By owing owes not, but still pays, at once
Indebted and discharged; what burden then?
O had his powerful destiny ordained
Me some inferior angel, I had stood
Then happy; no unbounded hope had raised
Ambition. Yet why not? some other power
As great might have aspired, and me though mean
Drawn to his part; but other powers as great
Fell not, but stand unshaken, from within
Or from without, to all temptations armed?

Satan's Address to the Sun.

Hadst thou the same free will and power to stand?
Thou hadst. Whom hast thou then, or what, to accuse,
But heaven's free love, dealt equally to all?
Be then his love accursed, since love or hate,
To me alike, it deals eternal woe.
Nay cursed be thou; since against his thy will
Chose freely what it now so justly rues.
Me miserable! which way shall I fly
Infinite wrath, and infinite despair?
Which way I fly is hell; myself am hell;
And, in the lowest deep, a lower deep
Still threatening to devour me opens wide,
To which the hell I suffer seems a heaven.
O then at last relent: is there no place
Left for repentance, none for pardon left?
None left but by submission; and that word
Disdain forbids me, and my dread of shame
Among the spirits beneath, whom I seduced
With other promises, and other vaunts
Than to submit, boasting I could subdue
The Omnipotent. Ay me, they little know
How dearly I abide that boast so vain,
Under what torments inwardly I groan,
While they adore me on the throne of hell,
With diadem and sceptre high advanced,
The lower still I fall, only supreme
In misery: such joy ambition finds.
But say I could repent, and could obtain,
By act of grace, my former state; how soon

Would height recall high thoughts, how soon unsay
What feigned submission swore? ease would recant
Vows made in pain, as violent and void.
For never can true reconcilement grow,
Where wounds of deadly hate have pierced so deep:
Which would but lead me to a worse relapse,
And heavier fall: so should I purchase dear
Short intermission bought with double smart.
This knows my punisher: therefore as far
From granting he, as I from begging peace:
All hope excluded thus, behold in stead
Of us outcast, exiled, his new delight,
Mankind created, and for him this world.
So farewell hope, and with hope farewell fear;
Farewell remorse: all good to me is lost;
Evil be thou my good; by thee at least
Divided empire with heaven's King I hold,
By thee, and more than half perhaps will reign;
As man ere long, and this new world, shall know.

Ben Jonson.

Born 1574. Died 1637.

SONG TO CELIA.

Drink to me only with thine eyes,
    And I will pledge with mine;
Or leave a kiss but in the cup,
    And I'll not look for wine.
The thirst, that from the soul doth rise,
    Doth ask a drink divine:
But might I of love's nectar sup,
    I would not change for thine.

I sent thee, late, a rosy wreath,
    Not so much honouring thee,
As giving it a hope, that there
    It could not withered be.
But thou thereon didst only breathe,
    And sent it back to me:
Since when it grows, and smells, I swear,
    Not of itself, but thee.

William Cowper.

Born 1731. Died 1800.

BOADICEA.*

When the British warrior queen,
    Bleeding from the Roman rods,
Sought, with an indignant mien,
    Counsel of her country's gods,

Sage beneath the spreading oak
    Sat the Druid, hoary chief;
Every burning word he spoke
    Full of rage, and full of grief.

Princess! if our aged eyes
    Weep upon thy matchless wrongs,
'Tis because resentment ties
    All the terrors of our tongues.

Rome shall perish—write that word
    In the blood that she has spilt;
Perish, hopeless and abhorred,
    Deep in ruin as in guilt.

* Boadicea, Queen of the Iceni. When Britain was invaded by the Romans she was taken prisoner by them, and eventually poisoned herself.

Rome, for empire far renowned,
  Tramples on a thousand states;
Soon her pride shall kiss the ground—
  Hark! the Gaul is at her gates!

Other Romans shall arise,
  Heedless of a soldier's name;
Sounds, not arms, shall win the prize,
  Harmony the path to fame.

Then the progeny that springs
  From the forests of our land,
Armed with thunder, clad with wings,
  Shall a wider world command.

Regions Cæsar never knew
  Thy posterity shall sway;
Where his eagles never flew,
  None invincible as they.

Such the bard's prophetic words,
  Pregnant with celestial fire,
Bending as he swept the chords
  Of his sweet but awful lyre.

She, with all a monarch's pride,
  Felt them in her bosom glow:
Rushed to battle, fought, and died,
  Dying, hurled them at the foe

Ruffians, pitiless as proud,
    Heaven awards the vengeance due ;
Empire is on us bestowed,
    Shame and ruin wait for you.

James Thomson.

Born 1700. Died 1748.

A SUMMER'S DAY.

FROM THE SEASONS: SUMMER.

Now, flaming up the heavens, the potent Sun
Melts into limpid air the high-raised clouds,
And morning fogs, that hovered round the hills
In party-coloured bands; till wide unveiled
The face of Nature shines, from where Earth seems,
Far stretched around, to meet the bending Sphere.
  Half in a blush of clustering roses lost,
Dew-dropping Coolness to the shade retires;
There, on the verdant turf, or flowery bed,
By gelid founts and careless rills to muse;
While tyrant Heat, dispreading through the sky,
With rapid sway his burning influence darts
On man, and beast, and herb, and tepid stream.

A Summer's Day.

Who can unpitying see the flowery race,
Shed by the morn, their new-flushed bloom resign,
Before the parching beam? So fade the fair,
When fevers revel through their azure veins.
But one, the lofty follower of the Sun,
Sad when he sets, shuts up her yellow leaves,
Drooping all night; and, when he warm returns,
Points her enamoured bosom to his ray.
  Home, from his morning task, the swain retreats;
His flock before him stepping to the fold:
While the full-uddered mother lows around
The cheerful cottage, then expecting food,
The food of innocence and health! The daw,
The rook and magpie, to the grey-grown oaks
That the calm village in their verdant arms,
Sheltering, embrace, direct their lazy flight;
Where on the mingling boughs they sit embowered,
All the hot noon, till cooler hours arise.
Faint, underneath, the household fowls convene;
And, in a corner of the buzzing shade,
The house-dog, with the vacant greyhound, lies
Out-stretched and sleepy. In his slumbers one
Attacks the nightly thief, and one exults
O'er hill and dale; till, wakened by the wasp,
They starting snap. Nor shall the Muse disdain
To let the little noisy summer-race
Live in her lay, and flutter through her song:
Not mean though simple; to the Sun allied,
From him they draw their animating fire.

Waked by his warmer ray, the reptile young
Come winged abroad; by the light air upborne,
Lighter, and full of soul. From every chink,
And secret corner, where they slept away
The wintry storms; or rising from their tombs,
To higher life; by myriads, forth at once,
Swarming they pour; of all the varied hues
Their beauty-beaming parent can disclose.
Ten thousand forms, ten thousand different tribes,
People the blaze! To sunny waters some
By fatal instinct fly; where on the pool
They sportive wheel; or, sailing down the stream,
Are snatched immediate by the quick-eyed trout,
Or darting salmon. Through the green-wood glade
Some love to stray; there lodged, amused and fed,
In the fresh leaf. Luxurious, others make
The meads their choice, and visit every flower,
And every latent herb: for the sweet task,
To propagate their kinds, and where to wrap,
In what soft beds, their young yet undisclosed,
Employs their tender care. Some to the house,
The fold, and dairy, hungry, bend their flight;
Sip round the pail, or taste the curdling cheese:
Oft, inadvertent, from the milky stream
They meet their fate; or, weltering in the bowl,
With powerless wings around them wrapped, expire.

James Beattie.

Born 1735. Died 1803.

THE HERMIT.

At the close of the day, when the hamlet is still,
And mortals the sweets of forgetfulness prove,
When nought but the torrent is heard on the hill,
And nought but the nightingale's song in the grove:
'Twas thus, by the cave of the mountain afar,
While his harp rung symphonious, a hermit began;
No more with himself or with nature at war,
He thought as a sage, though he felt as a man.

" Ah! why, all abandoned to darkness and woe,
Why, lone Philomela, that languishing fall?
For spring shall return, and a lover bestow,
And sorrow no longer thy bosom enthral.
But if pity inspire thee, renew the sad lay,
Mourn, sweetest complainer, man calls thee to mourn;
O soothe him, whose pleasures like thine pass away:
Full quickly they pass—but they never return.

" Now gliding remote on the verge of the sky,
The Moon half-extinguished her crescent displays:
But lately I marked when majestic on high
She shone, and the planets were lost in her blaze.
Roll on, thou fair orb, and with gladness pursue

The path that conducts thee to splendour again.
But man's faded glory what change shall renew!
Ah, fool! to exult in a glory so vain!

" 'Tis night, and the landscape is lovely no more;
I mourn, but, ye woodlands, I mourn not for you;
For morn is approaching, your charms to restore,
Perfumed with fresh fragrance, and glittering with dew:
Nor yet for the ravage of winter I mourn;
Kind nature the embryo blossom will save.
But when shall spring visit the mouldering urn!
O when shall it dawn on the night of the grave!

" 'Twas thus by the glare of false science betrayed,
That leads, to bewilder; and dazzles, to blind;
My thoughts wont to roam, from shade onward to shade,
Destruction before me, and sorrow behind.
'O, pity, great Father of light,' then I cried,
'Thy creature, who fain would not wander from thee;
Lo, humbled in dust, I relinquish my pride:
From doubt and from darkness thou only canst free.'

" And darkness and doubt are now flying away;
No longer I roam in conjecture forlorn:
So breaks on the traveller, faint, and astray,
The bright and the balmy effulgence of morn.
See Truth, Love, and Mercy, in triumph descending,
And nature all glowing in Eden's first bloom!
On the cold cheek of Death smiles and roses are blending,
And beauty immortal awakes from the tomb."

Robert Burns.

Born 1759. Died 1796.

THE COTTER'S SATURDAY NIGHT.

My loved, my honoured, much respected friend! *
No mercenary bard his homage pays;
With honest pride, I scorn each selfish end:
My dearest meed, a friend's esteem and praise:
To you I sing, in simple Scottish lays,
The lowly train in life's sequestered scene;
The native feelings strong, the guileless ways;
What Aiken in a cottage would have been;
Ah! though his worth unknown, far happier there I
    ween.

November chill blaws loud wi' angry sugh;[1]
The shortening winter-day is near a close;
The miry beasts retreating frae the pleugh;
The blackening trains o' craws to their repose
The toil-worn Cotter frae his labour goes,
This night his weekly moil is at an end,
Collects his spades, his mattocks, and his hoes,

---

* The first verse is an inscription of the poem to Mr. Aiken of Ayr, a friend of the poet's.

[1] Rushing sound.

Hoping the morn in ease and rest to spend,
And weary, o'er the moor, his course does hameward
    bend.

At length his lonely cot appears in view,
Beneath the shelter of an aged tree;
The expectant wee-things, toddlin, stacher[1] thro',
To meet their Dad, wi' flichterin[2] noise an' glee.
His wee bit ingle, blinkin bonnily,
His clean hearth-stane, his thriftie wifie's smile,
The lisping infant prattling on his knee,
Does a' his weary carking cares beguile,
An' makes him quite forget his labour an' his toil.

Belyve,[3] the elder bairns come drapping in,
At service out, amang the farmers roun';
Some ca' the pleugh, some herd, some tentie[4] rin
A cannie errand to a neebor town:
Their eldest hope, their Jenny, woman grown,
In youthfu' bloom, love sparkling in her e'e,
Comes hame, perhaps, to shew a braw new gown,
Or deposite her sair-won penny-fee,
To help her parents dear, if they in hardship be.

Wi' joy unfeigned brothers and sisters meet,
An' each for other's welfare kindly spiers:
The social hours, swift-winged, unnoticed fleet;

---

[1] Stagger.   [2] Fluttering.   [3] By and by.   [4] Cautious.

Each tells the uncos[1] that he sees or hears;
The parents, partial, eye their hopeful years;
Anticipation forward points the view.
The mother, wi' her needle an' her shears,
Gars[2] auld claes look amaist as weel's the new;
The father mixes a' wi' admonition due.

Their master's an' their mistress's command,
The younkers a' are warned to obey;
An' mind their labours wi' an eydent[3] hand,
An' ne'er, tho' out o' sight, to jauk or play:
"An', oh! be sure to fear the Lord alway,
An' mind your duty, duly, morn and night!
Lest in temptation's path ye gang astray,
Implore his counsel and assisting might:
They never sought in vain that sought the Lord aright!"

But, hark! a rap comes gently to the door;
Jenny, wha kens the meaning o' the same,
Tells how a neebor lad cam o'er the moor,
To do some errands, and convoy her hame.
The wily mother sees the conscious flame
Sparkle in Jenny's e'e, and flush her cheek;
Wi' heart-struck anxious care, inquires his name,
While Jenny hafflins[4] is afraid to speak;
Weel pleased the mother hears, it's nae wild worthless
    rake.

[1] News. [2] Makes. [3] Diligent. [4] Half

Wi' kindly welcome Jenny brings him ben;
A strappan youth; he takes the mother's eye;
Blythe Jenny sees the visit's no ill ta'en;
The father cracks¹ of horses, pleughs, and kye.
The youngster's artless heart o'erflows wi' joy,
But, blate² and laithfu',³ scarce can weel behave;
The mother, wi' a woman's wiles, can spy
What makes the youth sae bashfu' an' sae grave;
Weel pleased to think her bairn's respected like the lave.⁴

O happy love! where love like this is found!
O heart-felt raptures! bliss beyond compare!
I've paced much this weary, mortal round,
And sage experience bids me this declare—
"If Heaven a draught of heavenly pleasure spare,
One cordial in this melancholy vale,
'Tis when a youthful, loving, modest pair,
In other's arms breathe out the tender tale,
Beneath the milk-white thorn that scents the evening
    gale!"

Is there, in human form, that bears a heart—
A wretch! a villain! lost to love and truth!
That can, with studied, sly, ensnaring art,
Betray sweet Jenny's unsuspecting youth?
Curse on his perjured arts! dissembling smooth!
Are honour, virtue, conscience, all exiled?
Is there no pity, no relenting ruth,

¹ Talks.   ² Bashful.   ³ Sheepish.   ⁴ The rest.

Points to the parents fondling o'er their child?
Then paints the ruined maid, and their distraction wild!

But now the supper crowns their simple board,
The halesome parritch, chief o' Scotia's food:
The soupe their only hawkie¹ does afford,
That 'yont the hallan² snugly chows her cood;
The dame brings forth in complimental mood,
To grace the lad, her weel-hained³ kebbuck,⁴ fell,
An' aft he's prest, an' aft he ca's it guid;
The frugal wifie, garrulous, will tell
How 'twas a towmond⁵ auld, sin' lint was i' the bell.⁶

The cheerfu' supper done, wi' serious face,
They, round the ingle, form a circle wide;
The sire turns o'er, wi' patriarchal grace,
The big ha'-Bible, ance his father's pride:
His bonnet reverently is laid aside,
His lyart haffets⁷ wearing thin an' bare;
Those strains that once did sweet in Zion glide,
He wales⁸ a portion with judicious care;
And "Let us worship God!" he says, with solemn
    air.

They chant their artless notes in simple guise;
They tune their hearts, by far the noblest aim:

¹ Cow.   ² Partition wall.   ³ Well-saved.   ⁴ Cheese.
⁵ A twelvemonth.   ⁶ Since the flax was in flower.
⁷ Grey locks.   ⁸ Chooses.

Perhaps "Dundee's" wild warbling measures rise,
Or plaintive "Martyrs," worthy of the name;
Or noble "Elgin" beets the heavenward flame,
The sweetest far of Scotia's holy lays:
Compared with these, Italian thrills are tame;
The tickled ears no heart-felt raptures raise;
Nae unison hae they with our Creator's praise.

The priest-like father reads the sacred page,
How Abram was the friend of God on high;
Or Moses bade eternal warfare wage
With Amalek's ungracious progeny;
Or how the royal Bard did groaning lie
Beneath the stroke of Heaven's avenging ire;
Or Job's pathetic plaint, and wailing cry;
Or rapt Isaiah's wild, seraphic fire;
Or other holy seers that tune the sacred lyre.

Perhaps the Christian volume is the theme,
How guiltless blood for guilty man was shed;
How He, who bore in Heaven the second name,
Had not on earth whereon to lay His head:
How His first followers and servants sped;
The precepts sage they wrote to many a land:
How he, who lone in Patmos banishèd,
Saw in the sun a mighty angel stand;
And heard great Babylon's doom pronounced by Heaven's command.

Then kneeling down, to Heaven's Eternal King,
The saint, the father, and the husband prays:
Hope "springs exulting on triumphant wing,"
That thus they all shall meet in future days:
There ever bask in uncreated rays,
No more to sigh, or shed the bitter tear,
Together hymning their Creator's praise,
In such society, yet still more dear;
While circling time moves round in an eternal sphere.

Compared with this, how poor Religion's pride,
In all the pomp of method, and of art,
When men display to congregations wide
Devotion's every grace, except the heart!
The Power, incensed, the pageant will desert,
The pompous strain, the sacerdotal stole;
But haply, in some cottage far apart,
May hear, well pleased, the language of the soul;
And in His book of life the inmates poor enrol.

Then homeward all take off their several way;
The youngling cottagers retire to rest:
The parent-pair their secret homage pay,
And proffer up to Heaven the warm request,
That He, who stills the raven's clamorous nest,
And decks the lily fair in flowery pride;
Would, in the way His wisdom sees the best,
For them, and for their little ones provide;
But chiefly, in their hearts with grace divine preside.

From scenes like these old Scotia's grandeur springs,
That makes her loved at home, revered abroad:
Princes and lords are but the breath of kings;
"An honest man's the noblest work of God:"
And certes, in fair virtue's heavenly road,
The cottage leaves the palace far behind;
What is a lordling's pomp? a cumbrous load,
Disguising oft the wretch of human kind,
Studied in arts of hell, in wickedness refined!

O Scotia! my dear, my native soil!
For whom my warmest wish to Heaven is sent!
Long may thy hardy sons of rustic toil
Be blest with health, and peace, and sweet content!
And, oh, may Heaven their simple lives prevent
From luxury's contagion, weak and vile!
Then, howe'er crowns and coronets be rent,
A virtuous populace may rise the while,
And stand a wall of fire around their much-loved Isle.

O Thou! who poured the patriotic tide
That streamed through Wallace's undaunted heart;
Who dared to nobly stem tyrannic pride,
Or nobly die, the second glorious part,
(The patriot's God, peculiarly Thou art,
His friend, inspirer, guardian, and reward!)
O never, never Scotia's realm desert;
But still the patriot, and the patriot-bard,
In bright succession raise, her ornament and guard!

Robert Tannahill.

Born 1774. Died 1810.

JESSIE, THE FLOWER O' DUMBLANE.

The sun has gane down o'er the lofty Benlomond,
    And left the red clouds to preside o'er the scene,
While lanely I stray in the calm simmer gloamin'
    To muse on sweet Jessie, the flower o' Dumblane.
How sweet is the brier, wi' its saft faulding blossom,
    And sweet is the birk, wi' its mantle o' green;
Yet sweeter and fairer, and dear to this bosom,
    Is lovely young Jessie, the flower o' Dumblane.

She's modest as ony, and blithe as she's bonny;
    For guileless simplicity marks her its ain;
And far be the villain, divested of feeling,
    Wha'd blight in its bloom the sweet flower o' Dumblane.
Sing on, thou sweet mavis, thy hymn to the e'ening,
    Thou'rt dear to the echoes of Calderwood glen;
Sae dear to this bosom, sae artless and winning,
    Is charming young Jessie, the flower o' Dumblane.

How lost were my days 'till I met wi' my Jessie,
    The sports o' the city seemed foolish and vain,
I ne'er saw a nymph I would ca' my dear lassie,

'Till charmed with sweet Jessie, the flower o' Dumblane.
Though mine were the station o' loftiest grandeur,
Amidst its profusion I'd languish in pain;
And reckon as naething the height o' its splendour,
If wanting sweet Jessie, the flower o' Dumblane.

John Logan.

Born 1748.   Died 1788.

THE BRAES OF YARROW.

Thy braes were bonny, Yarrow stream!
　When first on them I met my lover;
Thy braes how dreary, Yarrow stream!
　When now thy waves his body cover!
For ever now, O Yarrow stream!
　Thou art to me a stream of sorrow;
For never on thy banks shall I
　Behold my love, the flower of Yarrow.

He promised me a milk-white steed,
　To bear me to his father's bowers;
He promised me a little page,
　To 'squire me to his father's towers;

The Braes of Yarrow.

He promised me a wedding-ring,—
    The wedding-day was fixed to-morrow;—
Now he is wedded to his grave,
    Alas, his watery grave, in Yarrow!

Sweet were his words when last we met;
    My passion I as freely told him!
Clasped in his arms, I little thought
    That I should never more behold him!
Scarce was he gone, I saw his ghost;
    It vanished with a shriek of sorrow;
Thrice did the water-wraith ascend,
    And gave a doleful groan through Yarrow.

His mother from the window looked,
    With all the longing of a mother;
His little sister, weeping, walked
    The greenwood path to meet her brother:
They sought him east, they sought him west,
    They sought him all the forest thorough;
They only saw the cloud of night,
    They only heard the roar of Yarrow!

No longer from thy window look,
    Thou hast no son, thou tender mother!
No longer walk, thou lovely maid!
    Alas, thou hast no more a brother!
No longer seek him east or west,
    And search no more the forest thorough;

For, wandering in the night so dark,
   He fell a lifeless corse in Yarrow.

The tear shall never leave my cheek,
   No other youth shall be my marrow;
I'll seek thy body in the stream,
   And then with thee I'll sleep in Yarrow.

The tear did never leave her cheek,
   No other youth became her marrow;
She found his body in the stream,
   And now with him she sleeps in Yarrow.

James Grahame.

Born 1765. Died 1811.

SABBATH MORNING

FROM THE SABBATH.

How still the morning of the hallowed day!
Mute is the voice of rural labour, hushed
The ploughboy's whistle, and the milkmaid's song.
The scythe lies glittering in the dewy wreath
Of tedded grass, mingled with fading flowers,
That yester-morn bloomed waving in the breeze.

Sabbath Morning.

Sounds the most faint attract the ear,—the hum
Of early bee, the trickling of the dew,
The distant bleating, midway up the hill.
Calmness sits throned on yon unmoving cloud.
To him who wanders o'er the upland leas,
The blackbird's note comes mellower from the dale;
And sweeter from the sky the gladsome lark
Warbles his heaven-tuned song; the lulling brook
Murmurs more gently down the deep-worn glen;
While from yon lowly roof, whose curling smoke
O'ermounts the mist, is heard, at intervals,
The voice of psalms, the simple song of praise.

With dove-like wings, Peace o'er yon village broods:
The dizzying mill-wheel rests; the anvil's din
Hath ceased; all, all around is quietness.
Less fearful on this day, the limping hare
Stops, and looks back, and stops, and looks on man,
Her deadliest foe. The toil-worn horse, set free,
Unheedful of the pasture, roams at large;
And, as his stiff unwieldy bulk he rolls,
His iron-armèd hoofs gleam in the morning ray.

But chiefly Man the day of rest enjoys.
Hail, SABBATH! thee I hail, the poor man's day.
On other days, the man of toil is doomed
To eat his joyless bread, lonely; the ground
Both seat and board; screened from the winter's cold
And summer's heat by neighbouring hedge or tree;

But on this day, embosomed in his home,
He shares the frugal meal with those he loves;
With those he loves he shares the heart-felt joy
Of giving thanks to God,—not thanks of form,
A word and a grimace, but reverently,
With covered face and upward earnest eye.

William Motherwell.

Born 1797. Died 1835.

SONG OF THE DANISH SEA-KING.

Our bark is on the waters deep, our bright blades in
    our hand,
Our birthright is the ocean vast—we scorn the girdled
    land ;
And the hollow wind is our music brave, and none can
    bolder be
Than the hoarse-tongued tempest raving o'er a proud
    and swelling sea!

Our bark is dancing on the waves, its tall masts
    quivering bend
Before the gale, which hails us now with the hollo of
    a friend;

And its prow is sheering merrily the upcurled billow's foam,
While our hearts, with throbbing gladness, cheer old Ocean as our home!

Our eagle-wings of might we stretch before the gallant wind,
And we leave the tame and sluggish earth a dim mean speck behind;
We shoot into the untracked deep, as earth-freed spirits soar,
Like stars of fire through boundless space—through realms without a shore!

Lords of this wide-spread wilderness of waters, we bound free,
The haughty elements alone dispute our sovereignty;
No landmark doth our freedom let, for no law of man can mete
The sky which arches o'er our head—the waves which kiss our feet!

The warrior of the land may back the wild horse, in his pride;
But a fiercer steed we dauntless breast—the untamed ocean tide;
And a nobler tilt our bark careers, as it quells the saucy wave,
While the Herald storm peals o'er the deep the glories of the brave.

Hurrah! hurrah! the wind is up—it bloweth fresh
    and free,
And every cord, instinct with life, pipes loud its fearless
    glee ;
Big swell the bosomed sails with joy, and they madly
    kiss the spray,
As proudly, through the foaming surge, the Sea-King
    bears away !

Professor Wilson.

Born 1785.   Died 1854.

THE WIDOWED MOTHER.

Beside her babe, who sweetly slept,
A widowed mother sat and wept
    O'er years of love gone by ;
And as the sobs thick-gathering came,
She murmured her dead husband's name
    'Mid that sad lullaby.

Well might that lullaby be sad,
For not one single friend she had
    On this cold-hearted earth ;
The sea will not give back its prey—
And they were wrapt in foreign clay
    Who gave the orphan birth.

Steadfastly as a star doth look
Upon a little murmuring brook,
  She gazed upon the bosom
And fair brow of her sleeping son—
"O merciful Heaven! when I am gone
  Thine is this earthly blossom!"

While thus she sat—a sunbeam broke
Into the room; the babe awoke,
  And from his cradle smiled!
Ah me! what kindling smiles met there!
I know not whether was more fair,
  The mother or her child!

With joy fresh-sprung from short alarms,
The smiler stretched his rosy arms,
  And to her bosom leapt—
All tears at once were swept away,
And said a face as bright as day,—
  "Forgive me that I wept!"

Sufferings there are from nature sprung,
Ear hath not heard, nor poet's tongue
  May venture to declare;
But this as Holy Writ is sure,
"The griefs she bids us here endure
  She can herself repair!"

John Denham.

Born 1615. Died 1688.

THE THAMES.

FROM COOPER'S HILL.

My eye descending from the Hill, surveys
Where Thames among the wanton valleys strays.
Thames! the most loved of all the Ocean's sons,
By his old sire, to his embraces runs,
Hasting to pay his tribute to the sea,
Like mortal life to meet eternity;
Though with those streams he no resemblance hold,
Whose foam is amber, and their gravel gold:
His genuine and less guilty wealth to explore,
Search not his bottom, but survey his shore,
O'er which he kindly spreads his spacious wing,
And hatches plenty for the ensuing spring;
Nor then destroys it with too fond a stay,
Like mothers which their infants overlay;
Nor with a sudden and impetuous wave,
Like profuse kings, resumes the wealth he gave.
No unexpected inundations spoil
The mower's hopes, nor mock the ploughman's toil;
But godlike his unwearied bounty flows;
First loves to do, then loves the good he does.

Nor are his blessings to his banks confined,
But free and common as the sea or wind;
When he, to boast or to disperse his stores,
Full of the tributes of his grateful shores,
Visits the world, and in his flying towers
Brings home to us, and makes both Indies ours;
Finds wealth where 'tis, bestows it where it wants,
Cities in deserts, woods in cities, plants.
So that to us no thing, no place, is strange,
While his fair bosom is the world's exchange.
O could I flow like thee! and make thy stream
My great example, as it is my theme;
Though deep yet clear, though gentle yet not dull;
Strong without rage, without o'erflowing full.

Joseph Addison.

Born 1672. Died 1719.

A HYMN.

When all thy mercies, O my God!
  My rising soul surveys,
Transported with the view, I'm lost
  In wonder, love, and praise.

O how shall words, with equal warmth,
    The gratitude declare
That glows within my ravished heart!
    But Thou canst read it there.

Thy Providence my life sustained,
    And all my wants redrest,
When in the silent womb I lay,
    And hung upon the breast.

To all my weak complaints and cries
    Thy mercy lent an ear,
Ere yet my feeble thoughts had learned
    To form themselves in prayer.

Unnumbered comforts to my soul
    Thy tender care bestowed,
Before my infant heart conceived
    From whom these comforts flowed.

When in the slippery paths of youth
    With heedless steps I ran;
Thine arm, unseen, conveyed me safe,
    And led me up to man;

Through hidden dangers, toils, and deaths,
    It gently cleared my way;
And through the pleasing snares of vice,
    More to be feared than they.

A Hymn.

When worn with sickness, oft hast thou
    With health renewed my face;
And, when in sins and sorrows sunk,
    Revived my soul with grace.

Thy bounteous hand with worldly bliss
    Hath made my cup run o'er;
And, in a kind and faithful friend,
    Hath doubled all my store.

Ten thousand thousand precious gifts
    My daily thanks employ;
Nor is the least a cheerful heart,
    That tastes these gifts with joy.

Through every period of my life
    Thy goodness I'll proclaim;
And after death, in distant worlds,
    Resume the glorious theme.

When nature fails, and day and night
    Divide thy works no more,
My ever grateful heart, O Lord,
    Thy mercy shall adore.

Through all eternity to Thee
    A joyful song I'll raise;
For, oh! eternity's too short
    To utter all thy praise.

Alexander Pope.

Born 1688. Died 1744.

THE UNIVERSAL PRAYER.

FATHER of all! in every age,
   In every clime adored,
By saint, by savage, and by sage,
   Jehovah, Jove, or Lord!

Thou Great First Cause, least understood,
   Who all my sense confined
To know but this, that Thou art good,
   And that myself am blind;

Yet gave me, in this dark estate,
   To see the good from ill;
And binding Nature fast in Fate,
   Left free the human will.

What conscience dictates to be done,
   Or warns me not to do,
This, teach me more than hell to shun,
   That, more than heaven pursue.

What blessings thy free bounty gives,
  Let me not cast away;
For God is paid when Man receives,
  To enjoy is to obey.

Yet not to Earth's contracted span
  Thy goodness let me bound,
Or think Thee Lord alone of Man,
  When thousand worlds are round:

Let not this weak, unknowing hand
  Presume thy bolts to throw,
And deal damnation round the land,
  On each I judge thy foe.

If I am right, thy grace impart,
  Still in the right to stay;
If I am wrong, oh teach my heart
  To find that better way!

Save me alike from foolish pride,
  Or impious discontent,
At aught thy wisdom has denied,
  Or aught thy goodness lent.

Teach me to feel another's woe,
  To hide the fault I see;
That mercy I to others show,
  That mercy show to me.

Mean though I am, not wholly so,
    Since quickened by thy breath;
Oh lead me wheresoe'er I go,
    Through this day's life or death!

This day, be bread and peace my lot:
    All else beneath the sun,
Thou knowst if best bestowed or not,
    And let thy will be done.

To thee, whose Temple is all space,
    Whose altar, earth, sea, skies,
One chorus let all Being raise!
    All Nature's incense rise!

Thomas Tickell.

Born 1686. Died 1740.

ON THE DEATH OF ADDISON.

CAN I forget the dismal night that gave
My soul's best part for ever to the grave!
How silent did his old companions tread,
By midnight lamps, the mansions of the dead,
Through breathing statues, then unheeded things,
Through rows of warriors, and through walks of kings!

On the Death of Addison.

What awe did the slow solemn knell inspire;
The pealing organ, and the pausing choir;
The duties by the lawn-robed prelate paid;
And the last words, that dust to dust conveyed!
While speechless o'er thy closing grave we bend,
Accept these tears, thou dear departed friend.
Oh, gone for ever! take this long adieu;
And sleep in peace, next thy loved Montague.
To strew fresh laurels, let the task be mine,
A frequent pilgrim, at thy sacred shrine;
Mine with true sighs thy absence to bemoan,
And grave with faithful epitaphs thy stone.
If e'er from me thy loved memorial part,
May shame afflict this alienated heart;
Of thee forgetful if I form a song,
My lyre be broken, and untuned my tongue,
My grief be doubled from thy image free,
And mirth a torment, unchastised by thee.
 Oft let me range the gloomy aisles alone,
Sad luxury! to vulgar minds unknown,
Along the walls where speaking marbles show
What worthies form the hallowed mould below;
Proud names, who once the reins of empire held;
In arms who triumphed; or in arts excelled;
Chiefs, graced with scars, and prodigal of blood;
Stern patriots, who for sacred freedom stood;
Just men, by whom impartial laws were given;
And saints who taught, and led, the way to heaven;
Ne'er to these chambers, where the mighty rest,

Since their foundation, came a nobler guest;
Nor e'er was to the bowers of bliss conveyed
A fairer spirit or more welcome shade.

John Dyer.

Born 1698.   Died 1758.

FROM GRONGAR HILL.*

Ever charming, ever new,
When will the landskip tire the view!
The fountain's fall, the river's flow,
The woody valleys, warm and low;
The windy summit, wild and high,
Roughly rushing on the sky!
The pleasant seat, the ruined tower,
The naked rock, the shady bower;
The town and village, dome and farm,
Each give each a double charm,
As pearls upon an Ethiop's arm.
 See on the mountain's southern side,
Where the prospect opens wide,
Where the evening gilds the tide;
How close and small the hedges lie!
What streaks of meadows cross the eye!

* Grongar Hill is in the Vale of the Towy, South Wales: the scenery of the valley being celebrated in the poem.

A step, methinks, may pass the stream,
So little distant dangers seem:
So we mistake the Future's face,
Eyed through Hope's deluding glass:
As yon summits soft and fair,
Clad in colours of the air,
Which to those who journey near,
Barren, brown, and rough appear;
Still we tread the same coarse way,
The present's still a cloudy day.

O may I with myself agree,
And never covet what I see:
Content me with an humble shade,
My passions tamed, my wishes laid;
For while our wishes wildly roll,
We banish quiet from the soul:
'Tis thus the busy beat the air;
And misers gather wealth and care.

Now, even now, my joys run high,
As on the mountain-turf I lie:
While the wanton Zephyr sings,
And in the vale perfumes his wings;
While the waters murmur deep;
While the shepherd charms his sheep;
While the birds unbounded fly,
And with music fill the sky,
Now, even now, my joys run high.

Be full, ye courts; be great who will;
Search for Peace with all your skill:

Open wide the lofty door,
Seek her on the marble floor :
In vain ye search, she is not there :
In vain ye search the domes of Care !
Grass and flowers Quiet treads,
On the meads, and mountain-heads,
Along with Pleasure, close allied,
Ever by each other's side :
And often, by the murmuring rill,
Hears the thrush, while all is still,
Within the groves of Grongar Hill.

William Shenstone.

Born 1714. Died 1763.

DISAPPOINTMENT.

FROM A PASTORAL BALLAD.

Ye shepherds ! give ear to my lay,
   And take no more heed of my sheep ;
They have nothing to do but to stray,
   I have nothing to do but to weep.
Yet do not my folly reprove ;
   She was fair—and my passion begun ;
She smiled—and I could not but love :
   She is faithless—and I am undone.

Disappointment.

Perhaps I was void of all thought;
   Perhaps it was plain to foresee
That a nymph so complete would be sought
   By a swain more engaging than me.
Ah! love every hope can inspire,
   It banishes wisdom the while,
And the lip of the nymph we admire
   Seems for ever adorned with a smile.

She is faithless, and I am undone:
   Ye that witness the woes I endure,
Let reason instruct you to shun
   What it cannot instruct you to cure.
Beware how you loiter in vain
   Amid nymphs of an higher degree;
It is not for me to explain
   How fair and how fickle they be.

Alas! from the day that we met
   What hope of an end to my woes?
When I cannot endure to forget
   The glance that undid my repose.
Yet time may diminish the pain:
   The flower, and the shrub, and the tree,
Which I reared for her pleasure in vain,
   In time may have comfort for me.

The sweets of a dew-sprinkled rose,
   The sound of a murmuring stream

The peace which from solitude flows,
　Henceforth shall be Corydon's theme.
High transports are shown to the sight,
　But we are not to find them our own;
Fate never bestowed such delight
　As I with my Phillis had known.

O ye woods! spread your branches apace,
　To your deepest recesses I fly;
I would hide with the beasts of the chase,
　I would vanish from every eye.
Yet my reed shall resound through the grove
　With the same sad complaint it begun;
How she smiled, and I could not but love!
　Was faithless, and I am undone!

Mark Akenside.

Born 1721. Died 1770.

THE NIGHTINGALE.

But hark! I hear her liquid tone.
　Now, Hesper, guide my feet
Down the red marle with moss o'ergrown,
Through yon wild thicket next the plain,
Whose hawthorns choke the winding lane
　Which leads to her retreat.

The Nightingale.

See the green space: on either hand
   Enlarged it spreads around:
See, in the midst she takes her stand,
Where one old oak his awful shade
Extends o'er half the level mead
   Enclosed in woods profound.

Hark, how through many a melting note
   She now prolongs her lays:
How sweetly down the void they float!
The breeze their magic path attends:
The stars shine out: the forest bends:
   The wakeful heifers gaze.

Whoe'er thou art whom chance may bring
   To this sequestered spot,
If then the plaintive Syren sing,
O softly tread beneath her bower,
And think of heaven's disposing power,
   Of man's uncertain lot.

O think, o'er all this mortal stage,
   What mournful scenes arise:
What ruin waits on kingly rage:
How often virtue dwells with woe:
How many griefs from knowledge flow:
   How swiftly pleasure flies.

O sacred bird, let me at eve,
   Thus wandering all alone,

Thy tender counsel oft receive,
Bear witness to thy pensive airs,
And pity nature's common cares
Till I forget my own.

Samuel Johnson.

Born 1707. Died 1784.

FROM THE VANITY OF HUMAN WISHES.

LET observation, with extensive view,
Survey mankind, from China to Peru,
Remark each anxious toil, each eager strife,
And watch the busy scenes of crowded life ;
Then say how hope and fear, desire and hate,
O'erspread with snares the clouded maze of fate,
Where wavering man, betrayed by venturous pride
To tread the dreary paths without a guide,
As treacherous phantoms in the mist delude,
Shuns fancied ills, or chases airy good :
How rarely reason guides the stubborn choice,
Rules the bold hand, or prompts the suppliant voice :
How nations sink, by darling schemes oppressed,
When vengeance listens to the fool's request.
Fate wings with every wish the afflictive dart,

From the Vanity of Human Wishes.

Each gift of nature, and each grace of art,
With fatal heat impetuous courage glows,
With fatal sweetness elocution flows,
Impeachment stops the speaker's powerful breath,
And restless fire precipitates on death.
  But, scarce observed, the knowing and the bold,
Fall in the general massacre of gold;
Wide-wasting pest! that rages unconfined,
And crowds with crimes the records of mankind;
For gold his sword the hireling ruffian draws,
For gold the hireling judge distorts the laws;
Wealth heaped on wealth nor truth nor safety buys,
The dangers gather as the treasures rise.
  Let history tell where rival kings command,
And dubious titles shake the madded land,
When statutes glean the refuse of the sword,
How much more safe the vassal than the lord:
Low skulks the hind beneath the rage of power,
And leaves the wealthy traitor in the Tower,
Untouched his cottage, and his slumbers sound,
Though confiscation's vultures hover round.
  The needy traveller, serene and gay,
Walks the wild heath, and sings his toil away.
Does envy seize thee? crush the upbraiding joy,
Increase his riches and his peace destroy;
Now fears in dire vicissitude invade,
The rustling brake alarms, and quivering shade,
Nor light nor darkness bring his pain relief,
One shews the plunder, and one hides the thief.

Yet still one general cry the skies assails,
And gain and grandeur load the tainted gales;
Few know the toiling statesman's fear or care,
The insidious rival and the gaping heir.
  Once more, Democritus, arise on earth,
With cheerful wisdom and instructive mirth,
See motley life in modern trappings dressed,
And feed with varied fools the eternal jest:
Thou who couldst laugh where want enchained caprice,
Toil crushed conceit, and man was of a piece;
Where wealth unloved without a mourner died;
And scarce a sycophant was fed by pride;
Where ne'er was known the form of mock debate,
Or seen a new-made mayor's unwieldy state;
Where change of favourites made no change of laws,
And senates heard before they judged a cause;
How wouldst thou shake at Britain's modish tribe,
Dart the quick taunt, and edge the piercing gibe;
Attentive truth and nature to descry,
And pierce each scene with philosophic eye.
To thee were solemn toys or empty show,
The robes of pleasure and the veils of woe:
All aid the farce, and all thy mirth maintain,
Whose joys are causeless, or whose griefs are vain.

Robert Blair.

Born 1700. Died 1746.

DEATH.

FROM THE GRAVE.

Sure 'tis a serious thing to die! my soul,
What a strange moment must it be, when near
Thy journey's end, thou hast the gulf in view!
That awful gulf, no mortal e'er repassed
To tell what's doing on the other side.
Nature runs back, and shudders at the sight,
And every life-string bleeds at thoughts of parting;
For part they must: body and soul must part;
Fond couple; linked more close than wedded pair.
This wings its way to its almighty source,
The witness of its actions, now its judge;
That drops into the dark and noisome grave,
Like a disabled pitcher of no use.

If death were nothing, and nought after death;
If when men died, at once they ceased to be,
Returning to the barren womb of nothing,
Whence first they sprung, then might the debauchee
Untrembling mouth the heavens :—then might the
    drunkard
Reel over his full bowl, and, when 'tis drained,
Fill up another to the brim, and laugh

At the poor bugbear death :—then might the wretch
That's weary of the world, and tired of life,
At once give each inquietude the slip,
By stealing out of being when he pleased,
And by what way, whether by hemp or steel ;
Death's thousand doors stand open.—Who could force
The ill-pleased guest to sit out his full time,
Or blame him if he goes?—Sure he does well,
That helps himself as timely as he can,
When able.——But if there's an hereafter ;
And that there is, conscience, uninfluenced
And suffered to speak out, tells every man ;
Then must it be an awful thing to die :
More horrid yet to die by one's own hand.
Self-murder!—name it not : our island's shame,
That makes her the reproach of neighbouring states
Shall nature, swerving from her earliest dictate
Self-preservation, fall by her own act?
Forbid it heaven.—Let not, upon disgust
The shameless hand be fully crimsoned o'er
With blood of its own lord.—Dreadful attempt!
Just reeking from self-slaughter, in a rage
To rush into the presence of our Judge ;
As if we challenged him to do his worst,
And mattered not his wrath!—Unheard-of tortures
Must be reserved for such : these herd together ;
The common damned shun their society,
And look upon themselves as fiends less foul.
Our time is fixed, and all our days are numbered ;

How long, how short, we know not:—this we know,
Duty requires we calmly wait the summons,
Nor dare to stir till Heaven shall give permission:
Like sentries that must keep their destined stand,
And wait the appointed hour, till they're relieved.
Those only are the brave that keep their ground,
And keep it to the last. To run away
Is but a coward's trick: to run away
From this world's ills, that at the very worst
Will soon blow o'er, thinking to mend ourselves,
By boldly venturing on a world unknown,
And plunging headlong in the dark;—'tis mad;
No frenzy half so desperate as this.

William Whitehead.

Born 1715. Died 1785.

THE YOUTH AND THE PHILOSOPHER.

A GRECIAN youth, of talents rare,
Whom Plato's philosophic care
Had formed for virtue's nobler view,
By precept and example too,
Would often boast his matchless skill,
To curb the steed, and guide the wheel.

And as he passed the gazing throng,
With graceful ease, and smacked the thong,
The idiot wonder they expressed
Was praise and transport to his breast.
 At length, quite vain, he needs would show
His master what his art could do ;
And bade his slaves the chariot lead
To Academus' sacred shade.
The trembling grove confessed its fright,
The wood-nymphs startled at the sight,
The muses drop the learned lyre,
And to their inmost shades retire !
 Howe'er, the youth with forward air
Bows to the sage, and mounts the car.
The lash resounds, the coursers spring,
The chariot marks the rolling ring,
And gathering crowds, with eager eyes,
And shouts, pursue him as he flies.
 Triumphant to the goal returned,
With nobler thirst his bosom burned ;
And now along the indented plain,
The self-same track he marks again ;
Pursues with care the nice design,
Nor ever deviates from the line.
 Amazement seized the circling crowd ;
The youths with emulation glowed,
Even bearded sages hailed the boy,
And all, but Plato, gazed with joy.
For he, deep judging sage, beheld

With pain the triumphs of the field;
And when the charioteer drew nigh,
And, flushed with hope, had caught his eye:
Alas! unhappy youth, he cried,
Expect no praise from me (and sighed);
With indignation I survey
Such skill and judgment thrown away.
The time profusely squandered there
On vulgar arts beneath thy care,
If well employed, at less expense,
Had taught thee honour, virtue, sense,
And raised thee from a coachman's fate,
To govern men, and guide the state.

Thomas Warton.

Born 1728. Died 1790.

THE APPROACH OF SUMMER.

Hence, iron-sceptered Winter, haste
To bleak Siberian waste!
Haste to thy polar solitude;
   Mid cataracts of ice,
Whose torrents dumb are stretched in fragments rude,
   From many an airy precipice,

Where, ever beat by sleety showers,
Thy gloomy Gothic castle towers;
Amid whose howling aisles and halls,
Where no gay sunbeam paints the walls,
On ebon throne thou lovest to shroud
Thy brows in many a murky cloud.
 E'en now, before the vernal heat,
Sullen I see thy train retreat:
Thy ruthless host stern Eurus guides,
That on a ravenous tiger rides,
Dim-figured on whose robe are shown
Shipwrecks, and villages o'erthrown:
Grim Auster, drooping all with dew,
In mantle clad of watchet hue:
And cold, like Zemblan savage seen,
Still threatening with his arrows keen;
And next, in furry coat embost
With icicles, his brother Frost.
 Winter farewell! thy forests hoar,
Thy frozen floods delight no more;
Farewell the fields, so bare and wild!
But come thou rose-cheeked cherub mild,
Sweetest Summer! haste thee here,
Once more to crown the gladdened year.
Thee April blithe, as long of yore,
Bermudas' lawns he frolicked o'er,
With musky nectar-trickling wing,
(In the new world's first dawning spring),
To gather balm of choicest dews,

And patterns fair of various hues,
With which to paint in changeful dye,
The youthful earth's embroidery;
To cull the essence of rich smells
In which to dip his new-born bells;
Thee, as he skimmed with pinions fleet,
He found an infant, smiling sweet;
Where a tall citron's shade embrowned
The soft lap of the fragrant ground.
There on an amaranthine bed
Thee with rare nectarine fruits he fed;
Till soon beneath his forming care,
You bloomed a goddess debonair;
And then he gave the blessed isle
Aye to be swayed beneath thy smile:
There placed thy green and grassy shrine,
With myrtle bowered and jessamine:
And to thy care the task assigned
With quickening hand, and nurture kind,
His roseat infant-births to rear,
Till Autumn's mellowing reign appear.

Nathaniel Cotton.

Born 1707. Died 1788.

THE FIRESIDE.

Dear Cloe, while the busy crowd,
The vain, the wealthy, and the proud,
   In folly's maze advance;
Though singularity and pride
Be called our choice, we'll step aside,
   Nor join the giddy dance.

From the gay world we'll oft retire
To our own family and fire,
   Where love our hours employs;
No noisy neighbour enters here,
No intermeddling stranger near,
   To spoil our heartfelt joys.

If solid happiness we prize,
Within our breast this jewel lies,
   And they are fools who roam;
The world hath nothing to bestow,
From our own selves our bliss must flow,
   And that dear hut our home.

Of rest was Noah's dove bereft,
When with impatient wing she left
  That safe retreat, the ark ;
Giving her vain excursions o'er,
The disappointed bird once more
  Explored the sacred bark.

Though fools spurn Hymen's gentle powers,
We, who improve his golden hours,
  By sweet experience know,
That marriage, rightly understood,
Gives to the tender and the good,
  A paradise below.

Our babes shall richest comforts bring;
If tutored right they'll prove a spring
  Whence pleasures ever rise :
We'll form their minds with studious care,
To all that's manly, good, and fair,
  And train them for the skies.

While they our wisest hours engage,
They'll joy our youth, support our age,
  And crown our hoary hairs;
They'll grow in virtue every day,
And they our fondest loves repay,
  And recompense our cares.

No borrowed joys! they're all our own,
While to the world we live unknown,

Or by the world forgot:
Monarchs! we envy not your state,
We look with pity on the great,
    And bless our humble lot.

Our portion is not large, indeed,
But then how little do we need,
    For nature's calls are few!
In this the art of living lies,
To want no more than may suffice,
    And make that little do.

We'll therefore relish with content,
Whate'er kind Providence has sent,
    Nor aim beyond our power;
For, if our stock be very small,
'Tis prudence to enjoy it all,
    Nor lose the present hour.

To be resigned when ills betide,
Patient when favours are denied,
    And pleased with favours given;
Dear Cloe, this is wisdom's part,
This is that incense of the heart,
    Whose fragrance smells to heaven.

We'll ask no long-protracted treat,
Since winter-life is seldom sweet:
    But, when our feast is o'er,

Grateful from table we'll arise,
Nor grudge our sons, with envious eyes,
   The relics of our store.

Thus hand in hand through life we'll go;
Its checkered paths of joy and woe
   With cautious steps we'll tread;
Quit its vain scenes without a tear,
Without a trouble, or a fear,
   And mingle with the dead.

While conscience, like a faithful friend,
Shall through the gloomy vale attend,
   And cheer our dying breath;
Shall, when all other comforts cease,
Like a kind angel whisper peace,
   And smooth the bed of death.

Thomas Blacklock.

Born 1721. Died 1791.

ODE TO AURORA.

OF time and nature eldest born,
Emerge, thou rosy-fingered morn,
Emerge in purest dress arrayed,
And chace from Heaven night's envious shade,

That I once more may, pleased, survey,
And hail Melissa's natal day.

Of time and nature eldest born,
Emerge, thou rosy-fingered morn :
In order at the eastern gate
The hours to draw thy chariot wait;
Whilst zephyr, on his balmy wings,
Mild nature's fragrant tribute brings,
With odours sweet to strew thy way,
And grace the bland, revolving day.

But as thou lead'st the radiant sphere,
That gilds its birth, and marks the year,
And as his stronger glories rise,
Diffused around the expanded skies,
Till clothed with beams serenely bright,
All Heaven's vast concave flames with light ;
So, when, through life's protracted day,
Melissa still pursues her way,
Her virtues with thy splendour vie,
Increasing to the mental eye :
Though less conspicuous, not less dear,
Long may they Bion's prospect cheer ;
So shall his heart no more repine,
Blessed with her rays, though robbed of thine.

Charles Dibdin.

Born 1745. Died 1814.

TOM BOWLING.*

Here, a sheer hulk, lies poor Tom Bowling
 The darling of our crew;
No more he'll hear the tempest howling,
 For death has broached him to.
His form was of the manliest beauty,
 His heart was kind and soft,
Faithful, below, he did his duty,
 But now he's gone aloft.

Tom never from his word departed,
 His virtues were so rare,
His friends were many and true-hearted,
 His Poll was kind and fair:
And then he'd sing so blithe and jolly,
 Ah, many's the time and oft!
But mirth is turned to melancholy,
 For Tom is gone aloft.

Yet shall poor Tom find pleasant weather,
 When He, who all commands,

---

* This exquisite ballad was written by Dibdin on the death of an elder brother.

Shall give, to call life's crew together,
  The word to pipe all hands.
Thus Death, who kings and tars despatches,
  In vain Tom's life has doffed,
For, though his body's under hatches,
  His soul is gone aloft.

Robert Nicoll.

Born 1814. Died 1837.

WILD FLOWERS.

BEAUTIFUL children of the woods and fields!
  That bloom by mountain streamlets 'mid the heather,
  Or into clusters, 'neath the hazels, gather,—
Or where by hoary rocks you make your bields,
  And sweetly flourish on through summer weather—
          I love ye all!

Beautiful flowers! to me ye fresher seem
  From the Almighty hand that fashioned all,
  Than those that flourish by a garden-wall;
And I can image you, as in a dream,
  Fair, modest maidens, nursed in hamlets small :—
          I love ye all!

Wild Flowers.

Beautiful gems! that on the brow of earth
  Are fixed, as in a queenly diadem;
Though lowly ye, and most without a name,
Young hearts rejoice to see your buds come forth,
  As light erewhile into the world came,—
      I love ye all!

Beautiful things ye are, where'er ye grow!
  The wild red rose—the speedwell's peeping eyes—
  Our own bluebell—the daisy, that doth rise
Wherever sunbeams fall or winds do blow;
  And thousands more, of blessed forms and dyes,—
      I love ye all!

Beautiful nurslings of the early dew!
  Fanned in your loveliness, by every breeze,
  And shaded o'er by green and arching trees:
I often wish that I were one of you,
  Dwelling afar upon the grassy leas,—
      I love ye all!

Beautiful watchers! day and night ye wake!
  The evening star grows dim and fades away,
  And morning comes and goes, and then the day
Within the arms of night its rest doth take;
  But ye are watchful wheresoe'er we stray,—
      I love ye all!

Beautiful objects of the wild-bee's love!
  The wild-bird joys your opening bloom to see,

And in your native woods and wilds to be.
All hearts, to nature true, ye strangely move ;
Ye are so passing fair—so passing free,—
       I love ye all !

Beautiful children of the glen and dell—
 The dingle deep—the moorland stretching wide,
And of the mossy fountain's sedgy side !
Ye o'er my heart have thrown a lovesome spell ;
 And, though the worldling, scorning, may deride,—
       I love ye all !

Matthew Gregory Lewis.[*]

Born 1773. Died 1818.

ALONZO THE BRAVE AND THE FAIR IMOGENE.

A WARRIOR so bold and a virgin so bright,
 Conversed as they sat on the green ;
They gazed on each other with tender delight:
Alonzo the Brave was the name of the knight—
 The maiden's, the Fair Imogene.

[*] Generally known as "Monk" Lewis from his well-known romance called "The Monk."

"And oh!" said the youth, "since to-morrow I go,
  To fight in a far distant land,
Your tears for my absence soon ceasing to flow,
Some other will court you, and you will bestow
  On a wealthier suitor your hand!"

"Oh! hush these suspicions," Fair Imogene said,
  "Offensive to love and to me;
For, if you be living, or if you be dead,
I swear by the Virgin that none in your stead
  Shall husband of Imogene be.

"If e'er, by caprice or by wealth led aside,
  I forget my Alonzo the Brave,
God grant that, to punish my falsehood and pride,
Your ghost at the marriage may sit by my side—
May tax me with perjury, claim me as bride,
  And bear me away to the grave!"

To Palestine hastened the hero so bold,
  His love she lamented him sore;
But scarce had a twelvemonth elapsed, when, behold!
A baron, all covered with jewels and gold,
  Arrived at Fair Imogene's door.

His treasures, his presents, his spacious domain,
  Soon made her untrue to her vows;
He dazzled her eyes, he bewildered her brain;
He caught her affections, so light and so vain,
  And carried her home as his spouse.

And now had the marriage been blest by the priest;
  The revelry now was begun;
The tables they groaned with the weight of the feast,
Nor yet had the laughter and merriment ceased,
  When the bell at the castle tolled—one.

Then first with amazement Fair Imogene found
  A stranger was placed by her side:
His air was terrific; he uttered no sound—
He spake not, he moved not, he looked not around—
  But earnestly gazed on the bride.

His vizor was closed, and gigantic his height,
  His armour was sable to view;
All pleasure and laughter were hushed at his sight;
The dogs, as they eyed him, drew back in affright;
  The lights in the chamber burned blue!

His presence all bosoms appeared to dismay;
  The guests sat in silence and fear;
At length spake the bride—while she trembled—"I pray,
Sir knight, that your helmet aside you would lay,
  And deign to partake of our cheer."

The lady is silent—the stranger complies—
  His vizor he slowly unclosed;
Oh, God! what a sight met Fair Imogene's eyes!
What words can express her dismay and surprise,
  When a skeleton's head was exposed!

All present then uttered a terrified shout,
  All turned with disgust from the scene;
The worms they crept in, and the worms they crept out,
And sported his eyes and his temples about,
  While the spectre addressed Imogene:—

"Behold me, thou false one, behold me!" he cried,
  "Remember Alonzo the Brave!
God grants that, to punish thy falsehood and pride,
My ghost at thy marriage should sit by thy side—
Should tax thee with perjury, claim thee as bride,
  And bear thee away to the grave!"

Thus saying, his arms round the lady he wound,
  While loudly she shrieked in dismay;
Then sunk with his prey through the wide-yawning ground,
Nor ever again was Fair Imogene found,
  Or the spectre that bore her away.

Not long lived the baron; and none, since that time,
  To inhabit the castle presume;
For chronicles tell that, by order sublime,
There Imogene suffers the pain of her crime,
  And mourns her deplorable doom.

At midnight, four times in each year, does her sprite,
  When mortals in slumber are bound,
Arrayed in her bridal apparel of white,

Appear in the hall with the skeleton knight,
And shriek as he whirls her around!

While they drink out of skulls newly torn from the grave,
    Dancing round them the spectres are seen;
Their liquor is blood, and this horrible stave
They howl:—"To the health of Alonzo the Brave,
    And his consort, the Fair Imogene!"

Michael Drayton.

Born 1563. Died 1631.

SUMMER'S EVE.

CLEAR had the day been from the dawn,
    All chequered was the sky,
Thin clouds, like scarfs of cobweb lawn,
    Veiled heaven's most glorious eye.

The wind had no more strength than this,
    That leisurely it blew,
To make one leaf the next to kiss,
    That closely by it grew.

The flowers, like brave embroidered girls,
    Looked as they most desired,

To see whose head with orient pearls
Most curiously was tyred.

The rills that on the pebbles played,
Might now be heard at will;
This world the only music made,
Else everything was still.

And to itself the subtle air
Such sovereignty assumes,
That it received too large a share
From nature's rich perfumes.

James Shirley.

Born 1594. Died 1666.

DEATH'S FINAL CONQUEST.

THE glories of our birth and state,
  Are shadows, not substantial things;
There is no armour against fate.
  Death lays his icy hands on kings;
    Sceptre and crown
    Must tumble down,
And in the dust be equal made
With the poor crooked scythe and spade.

Some men with swords may reap the field,
    And plant fresh laurels where they kill;
But their strong nerves at last must yield;
    They tame but one another still:
        Early or late
        They stoop to fate,
And must give up their murmuring breath,
When they, pale captives, creep to death.

The garlands wither on your brow,
    Then boast no more your mighty deeds;
Upon death's purple altar, now,
    See where the victor victim bleeds:
        All heads must come
        To the cold tomb,
Only the actions of the just
Smell sweet and blossom in the dust.

William Drummond.

Born 1585. Died 1649.

CHARITY.

COME, let us sound her praise abroad,
Sweet charity, the child of God!
Hers, on whose kind maternal breast
The sheltered babes of misery rest;

Who, when she sees the sufferer bleed,—
Reckless of name, or sect, or creed,—
Comes with prompt hand, and look benign,
To bathe his wounds in oil and wine;

Who in her robe the sinner hides,
And soothes and pities, while she chides;
Who lends an ear to every cry,
And asks no plea—but misery.

Her tender mercies freely fall,
Like heaven's refreshing dews on all;
Encircling in their wide embrace
Her friends—her foes—the human race.

Nor bounded to the earth alone,
Her love expands to worlds unknown;
Wherever faith's rapt thought has soared,
Or hope her upward flight explored.

Ere these received their name or birth,
She dwelt in heaven, she smiled on earth:
Of all celestial graces blessed,
The first—the last—the greatest—best.

When faith and hope, from earth set free,
Are lost in boundless ecstasy,
Eternal daughter of the skies,
She mounts to heaven—and never dies!

Robert Herrick.

Born 1591.   Died 1660.

TO DAFFODILS.

Fair daffodils, we weep to see
You haste away so soon;
As yet the early-rising sun
Has not attained his noon:
  Stay, stay,
Until the hastening day
  Has run
But to the even-song;
And having prayed together, we
Will go with you along!

We have short time to stay as you;
We have as short a spring;
As quick a growth to meet decay,
As you or any thing:
  We die,
As your hours do; and dry
  Away
Like to the summer's rain,
Or as the pearls of morning dew,
Ne'er to be found again.

Mary Robinson.
Born 1758. Died 1800.

THE SNOWDROP.

The snowdrop, winter's timid child,
    Awakes to life, bedewed with tears;
And flings around its fragrance mild,
And where no rival flowerets bloom,
Amid the bare and chilling gloom,
    A beauteous gem appears!

All weak and wan, with head inclined,
    Its parent breast the drifted snow;
It trembles while the ruthless wind
Bends its slim form; the tempest lowers,
Its emerald eye drops crystal showers
    On its cold bed below.

Poor flower! on thee the sunny beam,
    No touch of genial warmth bestows;
Except to thaw the icy stream,
Whose little current purls along
Thy fair and glossy charms among,
    And whelms thee as it flows.

The night-breeze tears thy silky dress,
    Which decked, with silvery lustre shone;
The morn returns, not thee to bless,

The gaudy crocus flaunts its pride,
And triumphs where its rival died,
   Unsheltered and unknown!

No sunny beam shall gild thy grave,
   No bird of pity thee deplore;
There shall no spreading branches wave;
For spring shall all her gems unfold,
And revel 'mid her buds of gold,
   When thou art seen no more!

Where'er I find thee, gentle flower,
   Thou still art sweet and dear to me;
For I have known the cheerless hour,
Have seen the sunbeams cold and pale,
Have felt the chilling wintry gale,
   And wept and shrunk like thee!

Charlotte Smith.

Born 1749.   Died, 1806.

TO THE SNOWDROP.

Like pendent flakes of vegetating snow,
   The early herald of the infant year,
Ere yet the adventurous crocus dares to blow,
   Beneath the orchard boughs thy buds appear.

While still the cold north-east ungenial lowers,
    And scarce the hazel in the leafless copse,
Or sallows shew their downy powdered flowers,
    The grass is spangled with thy silver drops.

Yet when those pallid blossoms shall give place
    To countless tribes, of richer hue and scent,
Summer's gay blooms, and autumn's yellow race,
    I shall thy pale inodorous bells lament.

So journeying onward in life's varying track,
    Even while warm youth its bright illusion lends,
Fond memory often with regret looks back
    To childhood's pleasures, and to infant friends.

Robert Fergusson.

Born 1751. Died 1774.

THE DELIGHTS OF VIRTUE.

Returning morn, in orient blush arrayed,
    With gentle radiance hailed the sky serene;
No rustling breezes waved the verdant shade;
    No swelling surge disturbed the azure main.

These moments, Meditation! sure are thine;
  These are the halcyon joys you wish to find,
When nature's peaceful elements combine
  To suit the calm composure of the mind.

The Muse, exalted by thy sacred power,
  To the green mountain's airy summit flew,
Charmed with the thoughtful stillness of an hour,
  That ushered beaming fancy to her view.

Fresh from old Neptune's fluid mansion sprung
  The sun, reviver of each drooping flower;
At his approach, the lark, with matin song,
  In notes of gratitude confessed his power.

So shines fair Virtue, shedding light divine
  On those who wish to profit by her ways;
Who ne'er at parting with their vice repine,
  To taste the comforts of her blissful rays.

She with fresh hopes each sorrow can beguile;
  Can dissipate adversity's deep gloom;
Make meagre poverty contented smile;
  And the sad wretch forget his hapless doom.

Sweeter than shady groves in Summer's pride,
  Than flowery dales or grassy meads, is she;
Delightful as the honeyed streams that glide
  From the rich labours of the busy bee.

Her paths and alleys are for ever green:—
  There innocence, in snowy robes arrayed,
With smiles of pure content, is hailed the queen
  And happy mistress of the sacred shade.

Oh let not transient gleams of earthly joy,
  From virtue lure your labouring steps aside;
Nor instant grandeur future hopes annoy
  With thoughts that spring from insolence and pride.

Soon will the wingèd moments speed away,
  When you'll no more the plumes of honour wear.
Grandeur must shudder at the sad decay,
  And pride look humble when he ponders there.

Deprived of virtue, where is beauty's power?
  Her dimpled smiles, her roses, charm no more;
So much can guilt the loveliest form deflower,
  We loathe that beauty which we loved before.

How fair are Virtue's buds, where'er they blow,
  Or in the desert wild or garden gay!
Her flowers how sacred, wheresoe'er they show
  Unknown to killing canker and decay!

Thomas Ken.

Born 1637.   Died 1711.

EVENING HYMN

ALL praise to thee, my God, this night,
For all the blessings of the light;
Keep me, oh, keep me, King of Kings,
Beneath thy own Almighty wings!

Forgive me, Lord, for thy dear Son,
The ill that I this day have done:
That with the world, myself, and thee,
I, ere I sleep, at peace may be.

Teach me to live, that I may dread
The grave as little as my bed;
To die, that this vile body may
Rise glorious at the judgment-day.

Oh! may my soul on thee repose,
And may sweet sleep mine eyelids close—
Sleep, that may me more vigorous make
To serve my God when I awake.

When in the night I sleepless lie,
My soul with heavenly thoughts supply;

Evening Hymn.

Let no ill dreams disturb my rest,
No powers of darkness me molest.

Dull sleep!—of sense me to deprive;
I am but half my time alive;
Thy faithful lovers, Lord, are grieved,
To lie so long of thee bereaved.

But though sleep o'er my frailty reigns,
Let it not hold me long in chains;
And now and then let loose my heart,
Till it an Hallelujah dart.

The faster sleep the senses bind,
The more unfettered are our minds;
Oh, may my soul from matter free,
Thy loveliness unclouded see!

Oh, when shall I, in endless day,
For ever chase dark sleep away;
And hymns with the supernal choir
Incessant sing, and never tire?

Oh, may my Guardian while I sleep,
Close to my bed his vigils keep;
His love angelical instil,
Stop all the avenues of ill.

Michael Bruce.

Born 1746. Died 1767.

ELEGY—WRITTEN IN SPRING

'Tis past: the iron north has spent his rage;
  Stern winter now resigns the lengthening day;
The stormy howlings of the winds assuage,
  And warm o'er ether western breezes play.

Of genial heat and cheerful light the source,
  From southern climes, beneath another sky,
The sun, returning, wheels his golden course:
  Before his beams all noxious vapours fly.

Far to the north grim winter draws his train,
  To his own clime, to Zembla's frozen shore;
Where, throned on ice, he holds eternal reign;
  Where whirlwinds madden, and where tempests roar.

Loosed from the bands of frost, the verdant ground
  Again puts on her robe of cheerful green—
Again puts forth her flowers; and all around,
  Smiling, the cheerful face of spring is seen.

Elegy—Written in Spring.

Behold! the trees new deck their withered boughs,
    Their ample leaves, the hospitable plane,
The taper elm, and lofty ash disclose;
    The blooming hawthorn variegates the scene.

The lily of the vale, of flowers the queen,
    Puts on the robe she neither sewed nor spun;
The birds on ground, or on the branches green,
    Hop to and fro, and glitter in the sun.

Soon as o'er eastern hills the morning peers,
    From her low nest the tufted lark upsprings
And, cheerful singing, up the air she steers;
    Still high she mounts, still loud and sweet she sings.

On the green furze, clothed o'er with golden blooms,
    That fill the air with fragrance all around,
The linnet sits, and tricks his glossy plumes,
    While o'er the wild his broken notes resound.

While the sun journeys down the western sky,
    Along the green sward, marked with Roman mound,
Beneath the blithesome shepherd's watchful eye,
    The cheerful lambkins dance and frisk around.

Now is the time for those who wisdom love,
    Who love to walk in virtue's flowery road,
Along the lovely paths of spring to rove,
    And follow nature up to nature's God.

Thus Zoroaster studied nature's laws;
    Thus Socrates, the wisest of mankind;
Thus heaven-taught Plato traced the Almighty cause,
    And left the wondering multitude behind.

Thus Ashley gathered academic bays;
    Thus gentle Thomson, as the seasons roll,
Taught them to sing the great Creator's praise,
    And bear their poet's name from pole to pole.

Thus have I walked along the dewy lawn;
    My frequent foot the blooming wild hath worn;
Before the lark I've sung the beauteous dawn,
    And gathered health from all the gales of morn.

And, even when winter chilled the aged year,
    I wandered lonely o'er the hoary plain:
Though frosty Boreas warned me to forbear,
    Boreas, with all his tempests, warned in vain.

Then, sleep my nights, and quiet blessed my days;
    I feared no loss, my mind was all my store;
No anxious wishes e'er disturbed my ease;
    Heaven gave content and health—I asked no more.

Now, spring returns: but not to me returns
    The vernal joy my better years have known;
Dim in my breast life's dying taper burns,
    And all the joys of life with health are flown.

Earl of Carlisle.

Born 1802.

TO A JESSAMINE TREE IN THE COURT OF NAWORTH CASTLE.

My slight and slender jessamine tree,
    That bloomest on my Border tower,
Thou art more dearly loved by me
    Than all the wreaths of foreign bower;
I ask not, while I near thee dwell,
    Arabia's spice, or Syria's rose;
Thy light festoons more freshly smell,
    Thy virgin white more purely glows.

My wild and winsome jessamine tree,
    That climbest up the dark gray wall,
Thy tiny flowerets seem in glee,
    Like silver spray-drops down to fall:
Say, did they from their leaves thus peep,
    When mailed moss-troopers rode the hill;
When helmèd warders paced the keep,
    And bugles blew for Belted Will?

My free and feathery jessamine tree,
    Within the fragrance of thy breath,

Yon dungeon grated to its key,
  And the chained captive sighed for death :
On Border fray, on feudal crime,
  I dream not, while I gaze on thee ;
The chieftains of that stern old time
  Could ne'er have loved a jessamine tree.

Robert Pollok.

Born 1799. Died 1827.

THE GENIUS OF BYRON.

FROM THE COURSE OF TIME.

He touched his harp, and nations heard, entranced.
As some vast river of unfailing source,
Rapid, exhaustless, deep, his numbers flowed,
And oped new fountains in the human heart.
Where Fancy halted, weary in her flight,
In other men, his, fresh as morning, rose,
And soared untrodden heights, and seemed at home,
Where angels bashful looked. Others, though great,
Beneath their argument seemed struggling whiles ;
He from above descending, stooped to touch
The loftiest thought ; and proudly stooped, as though
It scarce deserved his verse. With Nature's self

He seemed an old acquaintance, free to jest
At will with all her glorious majesty.
He laid his hand upon "the Ocean's mane,"
And played familiar with his hoary locks:
Stood on the Alps, stood on the Apennines,
And with the thunder talked as friend to friend;
And wove his garland of the lightning's wing,
In sportive twist, the lightning's fiery wing,
Which, as the footsteps of the dreadful God,
Marching upon the storm in vengeance, seemed;
Then turned, and with the grasshopper, who sung
His evening song beneath his feet, conversed.
Suns, moons, and stars, and clouds, his sisters were;
Rocks, mountains, meteors, seas, and winds, and storms,
His brothers, younger brothers, whom he scarce
As equals deemed. All passions of all men,
The wild and tame, the gentle and severe;
All thoughts, all maxims, sacred and profane;
All creeds, all seasons, Time, Eternity;
All that was hated, and all that was dear;
All that was hoped, all that was feared, by man,
He tossed about, as tempest-withered leaves;
Then, smiling, looked upon the wreck he made.
With terror now he froze the cowering blood,
And now dissolved the heart in tenderness;
Yet would not tremble, would not weep himself;
But back into his soul retired, alone,
Dark, sullen, proud, gazing contemptuously
On hearts and passions prostrate at his feet.

So Ocean, from the plains his waves had late
To desolation swept, retired in pride,
Exulting in the glory of his might,
And seemed to mock the ruin he had wrought.

Sir Henry Wotton.
Born 1568. Died 1639.

DESCRIPTION OF A HAPPY LIFE.

How happy is he born and taught
    That serveth not another's will;
Whose armour is his honest thought,
    And simple truth his utmost skill!

Whose passions not his masters are,
    Whose soul is still prepared for death,
Untied unto the worldly care
    Of public fame or private breath ;

Who envies none that chance doth raise,
    Or vice ; who never understood
How deepest wounds are given by praise,
    Nor rules of state, but rules of good.

Who hath his life from rumours freed,
    Whose conscience is his strong retreat ;

    Whose state can neither flatterers feed,
        Nor ruin make oppressors great;

Who God doth late and early pray
    More of his grace than gifts to lend;
And entertains the harmless day
    With a religious book or friend;

This man is freed from servile bands
    Of hope to rise, or fear to fall;
Lord of himself, though not of lands;
    And having nothing, yet hath all.

Sir John Davis.
Born 1570. Died 1626.

IMMORTALITY OF THE SOUL.

O IGNORANT poor man! what dost thou bear,
    Locked up within the casket of thy breast?
What jewels, and what riches hast thou there?
    What heavenly treasure in so weak a chest?

Look in thy soul, and thou shalt beauties find,
    Like those which drowned Narcissus in the flood:
Honour and pleasure both are in thy mind,
    And all that in the world is counted good.

Think of her worth, and think that God did mean,
  This worthy mind should worthy things embrace ;
Blot not her beauties with thy thoughts unclean,
  Nor her dishonour with thy passion base.

Kill not her quickening power with surfeitings :
  Mar not her sense with sensuality :
Cast not away her wit on idle things :
  Make not her free-will slave to vanity.

And when thou think'st of her eternity,
  Think not that death against her nature is ;
Think it a birth : and when thou goest to die,
  Sing like a swan, as if thou went'st to bliss.

And if thou, like a child, didst fear before,
  Being in the dark, where thou didst nothing see ;
Now I have brought thee torch-light, fear no more ;
  Now when thou diest, thou canst not hoodwinked be.

And thou, my soul, which turn'st with curious eye
  To view the beams of thine own form divine,
Now, that thou canst know nothing perfectly,
  While thou art clouded with this flesh of mine,

Take heed of over-weening, and compare
  Thy peacock's feet with thy gay peacock's train :
Study the best and highest things that are,
  But of thyself an humble thought retain.

Cast down thyself, and only strive to raise
  The glory of thy Maker's sacred name:
Use all thy powers that blessèd power to praise,
  Which gives thee power to be, and use the same.

Sir Thomas Wyatt.

Born 1503. Died 1542.

OF THE PAINS AND SORROWS CAUSED BY LOVE.

What meaneth this! when I lie alone
I toss, I turn, I sigh, I groan;
My bed meseems as hard as stone:
    What means this?
I sigh, I plain continually;
The clothes that on my bed do lie,
Always methink they lie awry;
    What means this?
In slumbers oft for fear I quake;
For heat and cold I burn and shake;
For lack of sleep my head doth ake;
    What means this?
A mornings then when I do rise,
I turn unto my wonted guise,
All day after muse and devise;
    What means this?

And if perchance by me there pass,
She unto whom I sue for grace,
The cold blood forsaketh my face;
    What means this?
But if I sit near her by,
With loud voice my heart doth cry,
And yet my mouth is dumb and dry;
    What means this?
To ask for help no heart I have;
My tongue doth fail what I should crave;
Yet inwardly I rage and rave;
    What means this?
Thus have I passèd many a year,
And many a day, though nought appear,
But most of that that most I fear;
    What means this?

Thomas Chatterton.

Born 1752.   Died 1770.

RESIGNATION.

O GOD, whose thunder shakes the sky,
  Whose eye this atom globe surveys;
To thee, my only rock, I fly,
  Thy mercy in thy justice praise.

Resignation.

The mystic mazes of thy will,
    The shadows of celestial light,
Are past the power of human skill—
    But what the Eternal acts is right.

Oh teach me in the trying hour,
    When anguish swells the dewy tear,
To still my sorrows, own thy power,
    Thy goodness love, thy justice fear.

If in this bosom aught but thee,
    Encroaching sought a boundless sway,
Omniscience could the danger see,
    And Mercy look the cause away.

Then why, my soul, dost thou complain?
    Why drooping seek the dark recess?
Shake off the melancholy chain,
    For God created all to bless.

But ah! my breast is human still;
    The rising sigh, the falling tear,
My languid vitals' feeble rill,
    The sickness of my soul declare.

But yet, with fortitude resigned,
    I'll thank the inflicter of the blow,
Forbid the sigh, compose my mind,
    Nor let the gush of misery flow.

The gloomy mantle of the night,
   Which on my sinking spirit steals,
Will vanish at the morning light,
   Which God, my East, my Sun, reveals.

Robert Southwell.

Born 1560. Died 1595.

CONSCIENCE.

My conscience is my crown;
   Contented thoughts my rest;
My heart is happy in itself:
   My bliss is in my breast.

Enough, I reckon wealth;
   A mean, the surest lot;
That lies too high for base contempt,
   Too low for envy's shot.

My wishes are but few,
   All easy to fulfil:
I make the limits of my power
   The bounds unto my will.

Conscience.

I have no hopes but one,
    Which is of heavenly reign:
Effects attained, or not desired,
    All lower hopes refrain.

I feel no care of coin;
    Well-doing is my wealth:
My mind to me an empire is,
    While Grace affordeth health.

I wrestle not with rage,
    While fury's flame doth burn
It is in vain to stop the stream,
    Until the tide doth turn.

But when the flame is out,
    And ebbing wrath doth end;
I turn a late enraged foe
    Into a quiet friend;

And taught with often proof,
    A tempered calm I find
To be most solace to itself,
    Best cure for angry mind.

No change of fortune's calms
    Can cast my comforts down:
When fortune smiles, I smile to think
    How quickly she will frown;

And when in froward mood,
She moved an angry foe,
Small gain I found to let her come,
Less loss to let her go.

William Julius Mickle.*

Born 1734. Died 1788.

THE MARINER'S WIFE.

And are ye sure the news is true?
And are ye sure he's weel?
Is this a time to think o' wark?
Make haste lay by your wheel;
Is this a time to spin a thread,
When Colin's at the door?
Reach down my cloak, I'll to the quay,
And see him come ashore.

* It is a disputed point as to whether or not this very popular song was written by Mickle. It is here inserted as Mickle's as it appears in all editions of his works, but many authorities assign the authorship to Jean Adams, a poor schoolmistress who resided at Greenock. The question is cleverly discussed in some prefatory remarks to the song in "The Book of Scottish Song," an admirable collection of Scotch ballads published by Messrs. Blackie and Son. The last stanza but one was interpolated by Dr. Beattie.

The Mariner's Wife.

For there's nae luck about the house,
    There's nae luck at a';
There's little pleasure in the house
    When our gudeman's awa.

And gie to me my bigonet,
    My bishop's satin gown;
For I maun tell the baillie's wife
    That Colin's in the town.
My Turkey slippers maun gae on
    My stockins pearly blue;
It's a' to pleasure our gudeman,
    For he's baith leal and true.

Rise, lass, and mak a clean fireside,
    Put on the muckle pot;
Gie little Kate her button gown
    And Jock his Sunday coat;
And mak their shoon as black as slaes,
    Their hose as white as snaw;
Its a' to please my ain gudeman,
    For he's been lang awa.

There's twa fat hens upo' the coop
    Been fed this month and mair;
Mak haste and thraw their necks about,
    That Colin weel may fare;
And mak our table neat and clean,
    Let every thing look braw,

For wha can tell how Colin fared
　　When he was far awa?

Sae true his heart, sae smooth his speech,
　　His breath like caller air;
His very foot has music in't
　　As he comes up the stair—
And shall I see his face again?
　　And shall I hear him speak?
I'm downright dizzy wi' the thought,
　　In troth I'm like to greet!

The cauld blasts o' the winter wind,
　　That thirl'd through my heart,
They're a' blawn by, I hae him safe,
　　Till death we'll never part;
But what puts parting in my head?
　　It may be far awa!
The present moment is our ain,
　　The neist we never saw.

Since Colin's weel, and weel content,
　　I hae nae mair to crave:
And gin I live to keep him sae,
　　I'm blest aboon the lave:
And will I see his face again?
　　And will I hear him speak?
I'm downright dizzy wi' the thought,
　　In troth I'm like to greet.

For there's nae luck about the house,
    There's nae luck at a';
There's little pleasure in the house
    When our gudeman's awa'.

Richard Lovelace.

Born 1618. Died 1658.

TO ALTHEA FROM PRISON.

WHEN Love with unconfinèd wings
    Hovers within my gates,
And my divine Althea brings
    To whisper at the grates;
When I lie tangled in her hair
    And fettered to her eye,
The birds that wanton in the air
    Know no such liberty.

When flowing cups run swiftly round
    With no allaying Thames,
Our careless heads with roses crowned,
    Our hearts with loyal flames;
When thirsty grief in wine we steep,
    When healths and draughts go free—
Fishes that tipple in the deep
    Know no such liberty.

When, like confinèd linnets, I
  With shriller throat shall sing
The sweetness, mercy, majesty
  And glories of my King;
When I shall voice aloud how good
  He is, how great should be,
Enlargèd winds, that curl the flood,
  Know no such liberty.

Stone walls do not a prison make,
  Nor iron bars a cage;
Minds innocent and quiet take
  That for an hermitage:
If I have freedom in my love
  And in my soul am free,
Angels alone, that soar above,
  Enjoy such liberty.

Henry Vaughan.

Born 1621. Died 1695.

EARLY RISING AND DEVOTION.

When first thy eyes unveil, give thy soul leave
To do the like; our bodies but forerun
The spirit's duty: true hearts spread and heave
Unto their God as flowers do to the sun;

Give Him thy first thoughts then, so shalt thou keep
Him company all day, and in Him sleep.

Let never sleep the sun up; prayer should
Dawn with the day: there are set lawful hours
'Twixt heaven and us; the manna was not good
After sun-rising; far day sullies flowers:
Rise to prevent the sun; sleep doth sins glut,
And heaven's gate opens when the world's is shut.

Walk with thy fellow-creatures: note the hush
And whisperings amongst them. Not a spring
Or leaf but hath his morning hymn; each bush
And oak doth know I AM.—Canst thou not sing?
O leave thy cares and follies! go this way,
And thou art sure to prosper all the day.

Serve God before the world; let him not go
Until thou hast a blessing; then resign
The whole unto him, and remember who
Prevailed by wrestling ere the sun did shine:
Pour oil upon the stones, weep for thy sin,
Then journey on, and have an eye to heaven.

Mornings are mysteries; the first, world's youth,
Man's resurrection, and the future's bud,
Shroud in their births; the crown of life, light, truth,
Is styled their star; the stone and hidden food:
Three blessings wait upon them, one of which
Should move—they make us holy, happy, rich.

When the world's up, and every swarm abroad,
Keep well thy temper, mix not with each clay;
Despatch necessities; life hath a load
Which must be carried on, and safely may:
Yet keep those cares without thee; let the heart
Be God's alone, and choose the better part.

Thomas Parnell.

Born 1679. Died 1717.

HYMN TO CONTENTMENT.

LOVELY, lasting peace of mind!
Sweet delight of human kind!
Heavenly-born, and bred on high,
To crown the fav'rites of the sky
With more of happiness below
Than victors in a triumph know!
Whither, oh! whither art thou fled,
To lay thy meek contented head?
What happy region dost thou please
To make the seat of calms and ease?
Ambition searches all its sphere
Of pomp and state to meet thee there.
Increasing avarice would find
Thy presence in its gold enshrined.

The bold adventurer ploughs his way,
Through rocks amidst the foaming sea,
To gain thy love? and then perceives
Thou wert not in the rocks and waves,
The silent heart which grief assails,
Treads soft and lonesome o'er the vales,
Sees daisies open, rivers run,
And seeks (as I have vainly done)
Amusing thought; but learns to know
That solitude's the nurse of woe.
No real happiness is found
In trailing purple o'er the ground;
Or in a soul exalted high,
To range the circuit of the sky;
Converse with stars above and know
All nature in its forms below:
The rest it seeks, in seeking dies,
And doubts at last, for knowledge, rise.
Lovely, lasting peace, appear
This world itself, if thou art here,
Is once again with Eden blessed,
And man contains it in his breast.

'Twas thus, as under shade I stood,
I sung my wishes to the wood,
And, lost in thought no more perceived
The branches whisper as they waved:
It seemed as all the quiet place
Confessed the presence of his Grace;

When thus she spoke :—" Go, rule thy will,
Bid thy wild passions all be still ;
Know God,—and bring thy heart to know
The joys which from religion flow :
Then every grace shall prove its guest,
And I'll be there to crown the rest ! "

Oh ! by yonder mossy seat,
In my hours of sweet retreat,
Might I thus my soul employ,
With sense of gratitude and joy,
Raised, as ancient prophets were,
In heavenly vision, praise, and prayer,
Pleasing all men, hurting none,
Pleased and blessed with God alone ;
Then while the gardens take my sight,
With all the colours of delight,
While silver waters glide along,
To please my ear, and court my song,
I'll lift my voice, and tune my string,
And thee, great Source of nature, sing.
The sun that walks his airy way,
To light the world, and give the day :
The moon, that shines with borrowed light ;
The stars, that gild the gloomy night ;
The seas that roll unnumbered waves ;
The wood that spreads its shady leaves ;
The field, whose ears conceal the grain,
The yellow treasure of the plain ;—

All of these, and all I see,
Should be sung, and sung by me:
They speak their Maker as they can,
But want and ask the tongue of man.
Go, search among your idle dreams,
Your busy or your vain extremes,
And find a life of equal bliss,
Or own the next begun in this.

Jonathan Swift.

Born 1667. Died 1745.

FROM A DESCRIPTION OF A CITY SHOWER.

CAREFUL observers may foretell the hour
(By sure prognostics) when to dread a shower;
While rain depends, the pensive cat gives o'er
Her frolics, and pursues her tail no more.
   *   *   *   *   *
   Meanwhile the South, rising with dappled wings,
A sable cloud athwart the welkin flings,
That swilled more liqour than it could contain,
And, like a drunkard, gives it up again.
Brisk Susan whips her linen from the rope,
While the first drizzling shower is borne aslope;
Such is that sprinkling, which some careless quean

Flirts on you from her mop—but not so clean:
You fly, invoke the gods; then turning, stop
To rail; she, singing, still whirls on her mop.
Not yet the dust had shunned the unequal strife,
But, aided by the wind, fought still for life,
And wafted with its foe by violent gust,
'Twas doubtful which was rain, and which was dust.
Ah! where must needy poet seek for aid,
When dust and rain at once his coat invade?
Sole coat, where dust cemented by the rain
Erects the nap, and leaves a cloudy stain!
  Now in contiguous drops the flood comes down,
Threatening with deluge this devoted town.
To shops in crowds the daggled females fly,
Pretend to cheapen goods, but nothing buy.
The Templar spruce, while every spout's a-broach,
Stays till 'tis fair, yet seems to call a coach.
The tucked-up seamstress walks with hasty strides,
While streams run down her oiled umbrella's sides.
Here various kinds, by various fortunes led,
Commence acquaintance underneath a shed.
Triumphant tories and desponding whigs,
Forget their feuds, and join to save their wigs.
Boxed in a chair the beau impatient sits,
While spouts run clattering over the roof by fits;
And ever and anon with frightful din
The leather sounds; he trembles from within.
So when Troy chairmen bore the wooden steed,
Pregnant with Greeks impatient to be freed

(Those bully Greeks, who, as the moderns do,
Instead of paying chairmen, run them through),
Laocoon struck the outside with his spear,
And each imprisoned hero quaked for fear.

William Falconer.

Born 1730. Died 1769.

OCEAN SCENE.

FROM THE SHIPWRECK.

The sun's bright orb, declining all serene,
Now glanced obliquely o'er the woodland scene.
Creation smiles around; on every spray
The warbling birds exalt their evening lay.
Blithe skipping o'er yon hill, the fleecy train
Join the deep chorus of the lowing plain;
The golden lime and orange there were seen,
On fragrant branches of perpetual green.
The crystal streams, that velvet meadows lave,
To the green ocean roll with chiding wave.
The glassy ocean hushed forgets to roar,
But trembling murmurs on the sandy shore:
And lo! his surface, lovely to behold!
Glows in the west, a sea of living gold!

While, all above, a thousand liveries gay,
The skies with pomp ineffable array.
Arabian sweets perfume the happy plains:
Above, beneath, around, enchantment reigns!
While glowing Vesper leads the starry train,
And night slow draws her veil o'er land and main,
Emerging clouds the azure east invade,
And wrap the lucid spheres in gradual shade,
While yet the songsters of the vocal grove,
With dying numbers tune the soul to love,
With joyful eyes the attentive master sees
The auspicious omens of an eastern breeze.
Round the charged bowl the sailors form a ring;
By turns recount the wondrous tale, or sing;
As love or battle, hardships of the main,
Or genial wine, awake the homely strain:
Then some the watch of night alternate keep,
The rest lie buried in oblivious sleep.

Deep midnight now involves the livid skies,
When infant breezes yet enervate rise,
The waning moon, behind a watery shroud,
Pale-glimmered o'er the long-protracted cloud.
A mighty ring around her silver throne,
With parting meteors crossed, portentous shone.
This in the troubled sky full oft prevails;
Oft deemed a signal of tempestuous gales.

George Herbert.

Born 1593. Died 1632.

THE FLOWER.

How fresh, O Lord, how sweet and clean
Are thy returns! even as the flowers in spring;
 To which, besides their own demean,
The late past frosts tributes of pleasure bring.
 Grief melts away like snow in May,
As if there were no such cold thing.

Who would have thought my shrivelled heart
Could have recovered greenness? It was gone
 Quite under ground; as flowers depart
To see their mother-root, when they have blown;
 Where they, together, all the hard weather,
Dead to the world, keep house unknown.

These are thy wonders, Lord of power,
Killing and quickening, bringing down to hell
 And up to heaven in an hour;
Making a chiming of a passing bell.
 We say amiss, this or that is:
Thy word is all, if we could spell.

O that I once past changing were,
Fast in thy Paradise, where no flower can wither!
   Many a spring I shoot up fair,
Offering at heaven, growing and groaning thither:
   Nor doth my flower want a spring shower;
My sins and I joining together.

   But while I grow in a straight line,
Still upwards bent, as if heaven were mine own,
   Thy anger comes, and I decline:
What frost to that? what pole is not the zone
   Where all things burn, when thou dost turn,
And the least frown of thine is shown?

   And now in age I bud again,
After so many deaths I live and write;
   I once more smell the dew and rain,
And relish versing: O my only light,
   It cannot be that I am he,
On whom thy tempests fell all night!

   These are thy wonders, Lord of love,
To make us see we are but flowers that glide:
   Which when we once can find and prove,
Thou hast a garden for us, where to bide.
   Who would be more, swelling through store,
Forfeit their Paradise by their pride.

Edmund Spenser.

Born 1553.   Died 1598.

PROCESSION OF THE SEASONS.

FROM THE FAIRIE QUEENE.

So forth issued the Seasons of the year;
First lusty Spring, all dight in leaves of flowers
That freshly budded, and new blooms did bear,
In which a thousand birds had built their bowers,
That sweetly sung to call forth paramours;
And in his hand a javelin he did bear,
And on his head (as fit for warlike stores)
A gilt engraven morion he did wear,
That as some did him love, so others did him fear.

Then came the jolly Summer, being dight
In a thin silken cassock coloured green,
That was unlined all, to be more light,
And on his head a garland well beseen
He wore, from which, as he had chaféd been,
The sweat did drop, and in his hand he bore
A bow and shafts, as he in forest green
Had hunted late the leopard or the boar,
And now would bathe his limbs with labour heated sore.

Then came the Autumn, all in yellow clad,
As though he joyed in his plenteous store,

Laden with fruits that made him laugh, full glad
That he had banished hunger, which before
Had by the belly often pinched him sore ;
Upon his head a wreath, that was enrolled
With ears of corn of every sort, he bore,
And in his hand a sickle he did hold,
To reap the ripened fruits the which the earth had yold.

Lastly came Winter, clothèd all in frieze,
Clattering his teeth for cold that did him chill,
Whilst on his hoary beard his breath did freeze,
And the dull drops that from his purpled bill
As from a limbeck did adown distil ;
In his right hand a tippèd staff he held,
With which his feeble steps he stayed still,
For he was faint with cold and weak with eld,
That scarce his loosèd limbs he able was to weld.

H. Howard, Earl of Surrey.

Born 1520. Died 1546.

DESCRIPTION OF SPRING.

The sweet season, that bud and bloom forth brings,
  With green hath clad the hill, also the vale ;
The nightingale with feathers new she sings ;
  The turtle to her mate hath told her tale

Summer is come, for every spray now springs;
The hart hath hung his old head on the pale;
The buck in brake his winter coat he flings:
The fishes fleet with new-repairèd scale;
The adder all her slough away she flings;
The swift swallow pursueth the flies small;
The busy bee her honey now she brings;
Winter is worn that was the flower's bale.
And thus I see, among these pleasant things,
  Each care decays, and yet my sorrow springs.

Thomas Carew.

Born 1589. Died 1639.

THE SPRING

Now that the winter's gone, the earth has lost
Her snow-white robes: and now no more the frost
Candies the grass, or casts an icy cream
Upon the silver lake or crystal stream:
But the warm sun thaws the benumbèd earth,
And makes it tender; gives a sacred birth
To the dead swallow; wakes in hollow tree
The drowsy cuckoo and the humble bee.—
Now do a choir of chirping minstrels bring,
In triumph to the world, the youthful Spring:

The valleys, hills, and woods, in rich array,
Welcome the coming of the longed-for May.
Now all things smile—only my love doth lower:
Nor hath the scalding noon-day sun the power
To melt that marble ice, which still doth hold
Her heart congealed, and makes her pity cold.
The ox, which lately did for shelter fly
Into the stall, doth now securely lie
In open fields; and love no more is made
By the fireside: but in the cooler shade
Amyntas now doth with his Chloris sleep
Under a sycamore, and all things keep
Time with the season—only she doth carry
June in her eyes, in her heart January.

George Crabbe.

Born 1754. Died 1852.

THE WIFE'S FUNERAL.

FROM THE PARISH REGISTER.

Then died, lamented, in the strength of life,
A valued mother, and a faithful wife:
Called not away, when time had loosed each hold
On the fond heart, and each desire grew cold;

But when, to all that knit us to our kind,
She felt fast bound, as charity can bind;—
Not when the ills of age, its pain, its care,
The drooping spirit for its fate prepare;
And, each affection failing, leaves the heart
Loosed from life's charm, and willing to depart:—
But all her ties the strong invader broke,
In all their strength, by one tremendous stroke!
Sudden and swift the eager pest came on,
And terror grew, till every hope was gone,
Still those around appeared for hope to seek:
But viewed the sick, and were afraid to speak.

 Slowly they bore, with solemn step, the dead;
When grief grew loud, and bitter tears were shed,
My part began: a crowd drew near the place,
Awe in each eye, alarm in every face;
So swift the ill, and of so fierce a kind,
That fear with pity mingled in each mind;
Friends with the husband came, their griefs to blend;
For good-man Frankford was to all a friend.
The last-born boy they held above the bier;
He knew not grief, but cries expressed his fear;
Each different age and sex revealed its pain,
In now a louder, now a lower strain!
While the meek father, listening to their tones,
Swelled the full cadence of the grief by groans.

 The elder sister strove her pangs to hide,
And soothing words to younger minds applied:

"Be still, be patient;" oft she strove to stay
But failed as oft, and weeping turned away.
  Curious and sad, upon the fresh-dug hill,
The village lads stood melancholy still;
And idle children, wandering to and fro,
As nature guided, took the tone of woe.
  Arrived at home, how then they gazed around.
In every place—where she—no more was found:—
The seat at table she was wont to fill;
The fire-side chair, still set, but vacant still;
The garden-walks, a labour all her own;
The latticed bower, with trailing shrubs o'ergrown;
The Sunday pew she filled with all her race,—
Each place of hers was now a sacred place:
That, while it called up sorrows in the eyes,
Pierced the full heart, and forced them still to rise.
Oh sacred sorrow! by whom souls are tried,
Sent not to punish mortals, but to guide;
If thou art mine (and who shall proudly dare
To tell his Maker, he has had a share?)
Still let me feel for what thy pangs are sent,
And be my guide, and not my punishment!

Isaac Watts.

Born 1674. Died 1748.

EARTH AND HEAVEN.

Hast thou not seen, impatient boy?
　Hast thou not read the solemn truth,
That gray experience writes for giddy youth
　　On every mortal joy!
　　Pleasure must be dashed with pain:
　　And yet, with heedless haste,
　　The thirsty boy repeats the taste,
Nor hearkens to despair, but tries the bowl again.
The rills of pleasure never run sincere:
　　Earth has no unpolluted spring,
From the cursed soil some dangerous taint they bear;
So roses grow on thorns, and honey wears a sting.

In vain we seek a heaven below the sky;
　The world has false but fluttering charms;
Its distant joys shew big in our esteem,
But lessen still as they draw near the eye:
　　In our embrace the visions die:
　　And when we grasp the airy forms,
　　　We lose the pleasing dream.

Earth, with her scenes of gay delight,
Is but a landscape rudely drawn,

With glaring colours, and false light;
Distance commends it to the sight,
  For fools to gaze upon,
But bring the nauseous daubing nigh,
Coarse and confused the hideous figures lie,
Dissolve the pleasure, and offend the eye.

Look up, my soul, pant toward the eternal hills;
  Those heavens are fairer than they seem;
There pleasures all sincere glide on in crystal rills.
  There not a dreg of guilt defiles,
    Nor grief disturbs the stream.
  That Canaan knows no noxious thing,
    No cursèd soil, no taintèd spring,
Nor roses grow on thorns, nor honey wears a sting.

Andrew Marvell.

Born 1620. Died 1678.

FROM THE NYMPH'S COMPLAINT FOR THE DEATH OF HER FAWN.

With sweetest milk and sugar, first
I it at mine own fingers nursed;
And as it grew so every day
It waxed more white and sweet than they,

It had so sweet a breath! and oft
I blushed to see its foot more soft,
And white, shall I say? than my hand—
Than any lady's of the land.

It was a wondrous thing how fleet
'Twas on those little silver feet.
With what a pretty skipping grace
It oft would challenge me the race;
And when 't had left me far away,
'Twould stay, and run again, and stay.
For it was nimbler much than hinds,
And trod as if on the four winds.

I have a garden of my own,
But so with roses overgrown,
And lilies, that you would it guess
To be a little wilderness;
And all the spring time of the year
It loved only to be there.
Among the beds of lilies I
Have sought it oft, where it should lie;
Yet could not, till itself would rise,
Find it although before mine eyes;
For in the flaxen lilies' shade,
It like a bank of lilies laid.
Upon the roses it would feed,
Until its lips e'en seemed to bleed;
And then to me 't would boldly trip,

And print those roses on my lip,
But all its chief delight was still
On roses thus itself to fill;
And its pure virgin lips to fold
In whitest sheets of lilies cold.
Had it lived long, it would have been
Lilies without roses within.

James Russell Lowell.

Born 1819.

THE FORLORN.

The night is dark, the stinging sleet,
    Swept by the bitter gusts of air,
Drives whistling down the lonely street,
    And stiffens on the pavement bare.

The street-lamps flare and struggle dim
    Through the white sleet-clouds as they pass,
Or, governed by a boisterous whim,
    Drop down and rattle on the glass.

One poor, heart-broken, outcast girl
    Faces the east-wind's searching flaws,
And, as about her heart they whirl,
    Her tattered cloak more tightly draws.

The flat brick walls look cold and bleak,
　　Her bare feet to the sidewalk freeze;
Yet dares she not a shelter seek,
　　Though faint with hunger and disease.

The sharp storm cuts her forehead bare,
　　And, piercing through her garments thin,
Beats on her shrunken breast, and there
　　Makes colder the cold heart within.

She lingers where a ruddy glow
　　Streams outward through an open shutter,
Giving more bitterness to woe,
　　More loneliness to desertion utter.

One half the cold she had not felt,
　　Until she saw this gush of light
Spread warmly forth, and seem to melt
　　Its slow way through the deadening night.

She hears a woman's voice within,
　　Singing sweet words her childhood knew,
And years of misery and sin
　　Furl off, and leave her heaven blue.

Her freezing heart, like one who sinks
　　Outwearied in the drifting snow,
Drowses to deadly sleep and thinks
　　No longer of its hopeless woe:

Q

Old fields, and clear blue summer days,
    Old meadows, green with grass and trees,
That shimmer through the trembling haze
    And whiten in the western breeze,—

Old faces,—all the friendly past
    Rises within her heart again,
And sunshine from her childhood cast
    Makes summer of the icy rain.

Enhaloed by a mild, warm glow,
    From all humanity apart,
She hears old footsteps wandering slow
    Through the lone chambers of her heart.

Outside the porch before the door,
    Her cheek upon the cold, hard stone,
She lies, no longer foul and poor,
    No longer dreary and alone.

Next morning something heavily
    Against the opening door did weigh,
And there, from sin and sorrow free,
    A woman on the threshold lay.

A smile upon the wan lips told
    That she had found a calm release,
And that, from out the want and cold,
    The song had borne her soul in peace.

For, whom the heart of man shuts out,
    Straightway the heart of God takes in,
And fences them all round about
    With silence mid the world's loud din;

And one of his great charities
    Is Music, and it doth not scorn
To close the lids upon the eyes
    Of the polluted and forlorn;

Far was she from her childhood's home,
    Farther in guilt had wandered thence,
Yet thither it had bid her come
    To die in maiden innocence.

Abraham Cowley.

Born 1618. Died 1667.

THE SHORTNESS OF LIFE AND UNCERTAINTY OF RICHES.

Why dost thou heap up wealth, which thou must quit,
Or, what is worse, be left by it?
Why dost thou load thyself when thou'rt to fly,
O man! ordained to die?

Why dost thou build up stately rooms on high,
Thou who art under ground to lie?
Thou sowest, and plant'st, but no fruit must see,
For death, alas! is reaping thee.

Suppose thou fortune couldst to tameness bring,
And clip or pinion her wing;
Suppose thou couldst on fate so far prevail,
As not to cut off thy entail;

Yet death at all that subtlety will laugh;
Death will that foolish gardener mock,
Who does a slight and annual plant ingraff
Upon a lasting stock.

Thou dost thyself wise and industrious deem;
A mighty husband thou wouldst seem;
Fond man! like a bought slave, thou all the while
Dost but for others sweat and toil.

Officious fool! that needs must meddling be
In business that concerns not thee;
For when to future years thou extend'st thy cares,
Thou deal'st in other men's affairs.

Even aged men, as if they truly were
Children again, for age prepare;
Provisions for long travel they design,
In the last point of their short line.

The Shortness of Life.

Wisely the ant against poor winter hoards
The stock which summer's wealth affords;
In grasshoppers, which must at autumn die,
How vain were such an industry!

Of power and honour the deceitful light
Might half excuse our cheated sight;
If it of life the whole small time would stay
And be our sunshine all the day.

Like lightning that begot but in a cloud
(Though shining bright and speaking loud),
Whilst it begins, concludes its violent race,
And where it gilds it wounds the place.

Oh scene of fortune, which dost fair appear
Only to men that stand not near!
Proud, Poverty, that tinsel bravery wears,
And, like a rainbow, painted tears!

Be prudent, and the shore in prospect keep;
In a weak boat trust not the deep;
Placed beneath envy, above envying rise;
Pity great men, great things despise.

The wise example of the heavenly lark,
Thy fellow-poet, Cowley! mark;
Above the clouds let thy proud music sound;
Thy humble nest build on the ground.

John Gay.
Born 1688. Died 1732.

BLACK-EYED SUSAN.

ALL in the Downs the fleet was moored,
   The streamers waving in the wind,
When black-eyed Susan came aboard ;
   "O! where shall I my true-love find?
Tell me, ye jovial sailors, tell me true
If my sweet William sails among the crew."

William, who high upon the yard,
   Rocked with the billow to and fro,
Soon as her well-known voice he heard,
   He sighed, and cast his eyes below :
The cord slides swiftly through his glowing hands,
And quick as lightning on the deck he stands.

So the sweet lark, high poised in air,
   Shuts close his pinions to his breast,
If chance his mate's shrill call he hear,
   And drops at once into her nest :—
The noblest captain in the British fleet
Might envy William's lip those kisses sweet.

"O Susan, Susan, lovely dear,
   My vows shall ever true remain ;

Let me kiss off that falling tear;
   We only part to meet again.
Change as ye list, ye winds; my heart shall be
The faithful compass that still points to thee.

"Believe not what the landmen say,
   Who tempt with doubts thy constant mind:
They'll tell thee, sailors, when away,
   In every port a sweetheart find:
Yes, yes, believe them when they tell thee so,
For thou art present wheresoe'er I go.

"If to fair India's coast we sail,
   Thy eyes are seen in diamonds bright,
Thy breath is Afric's spicy gale,
   Thy skin is ivory so white.
Thus every beauteous object that I view
Wakes in my soul some charm of lovely Sue.

"Though battle call me from thy arms,
   Let not my pretty Susan mourn;
Though cannons roar, yet safe from harms
   William shall to his dear return.
Love turns aside the balls that round me fly,
Lest precious tears should drop from Susan's eye."

The boatswain gave the dreadful word,
   The sails their swelling bosom spread;

No longer must she stay aboard;
  They kissed, she sighed, he hung his head.
Her lessening boat unwilling rows to land;
"Adieu!" she cries; and waved her lily hand.

John Lyly.

Born 1553. Died 1600.

CUPID AND CAMPASPE.

Cupid and my Campaspe played
At cards for kisses; Cupid paid:
He stakes his quiver, bow and arrows,
His mother's doves, and team of sparrows;
Loses them, too; then down he throws
The coral of his lip, the rose
Growing on's cheek (but none knows how),
With these the crystal of his brow,
And then the dimple of his chin;
All these did my Campaspe win.
At last he set her both his eyes,
She won, and Cupid blind did rise.
  O Love! has she done this to thee?
  What shall, alas! become of me?

William Habington.

Born 1605. Died 1645.

THE FIRMAMENT.

When I survey the bright
    Celestial sphere,
So rich with jewels hung, that night
Doth like an Ethiop bride appear;

My soul her wings doth spread,
    And heaven-ward flies,
The Almighty's mysteries to read
In the large volumes of the skies.

For the bright firmament
    Shoots forth no flame
So silent, but is eloquent
In speaking the Creator's name.

No unregarded star
    Contracts its light
Into so small a character
Removed far from our human sight:

But if we steadfast look,
    We shall discern
In it, as in some holy book,
How man may heavenly knowledge learn.

Christopher Marlowe.

Born 1561. Died 1593.

THE PASSIONATE SHEPHERD TO HIS LOVE.

Come live with me and be my Love,
And we will all the pleasures prove
That hills and valleys, dale and field,
And all the craggy mountains yield.

There will we sit upon the rocks
And see the shepherds feed their flocks,
By shallow rivers, to whose falls
Melodious birds sing madrigals.

There will I make thee beds of roses
And a thousand fragrant posies,
A cap of flowers, and a kirtle
Embroidered all with leaves of myrtle.

A gown made of the finest wool,
Which from our pretty lambs we pull,
Fair linèd slippers for the cold,
With buckles of the purest gold.

A belt of straw and ivy buds
With coral clasps and amber studs:

And if these pleasures may thee move,
Come live with me and be my Love.

Thy silver dishes for thy meat
As precious as the gods do eat,
Shall on an ivory table be
Prepared each day for thee and me.

The shepherd swains shall dance and sing
For thy delight each May-morning:
If these delights thy mind may move,
Then live with me and be my Love.

Matthew Prior.
Born 1664. Died 1721.

CHARITY.

Did sweeter sounds adorn my flowing tongue,
Than ever man pronounced, or angel sung:
Had I all knowledge, human and divine,
That thought can reach, or science can define;
And had I power to give that knowledge birth,
In all the speeches of the babbling earth:
Did Shadrach's zeal my glowing breast inspire,
To weary tortures, and rejoice in fire:
Or had I faith like that which Israel saw,

When Moses gave them miracles, and law:
Yet, gracious Charity, indulgent guest,
Were not thy power exerted in my breast;
Those speeches would send up unheeded prayer:
That scorn of life would be but wild despair:
A tymbal's sound were better than my voice:
My faith were form: my eloquence were noise.

Charity, decent, modest, easy, kind,
Softens the high, and rears the abject mind;
Knows with just reins, and gentle hand to guide,
Betwixt vile shame, and arbitrary pride.
Not soon provoked, she easily forgives;
And much she suffers, as she much believes.
Soft peace she brings wherever she arrives:
She builds our quiet, as she forms our lives;
Lays the rough paths of peevish nature even;
And opens in each heart a little heaven.

Each other gift, which God on man bestows,
Its proper bounds, and due reflection knows;
To one fixt purpose dedicates its power;
And finishing its act, exists no more.
Thus, in obedience to what heaven decrees,
Knowledge shall fail, and prophecy shall cease:
But lasting Charity's more ample sway,
Nor bound by Time, nor subject to decay,
In happy triumph shall for ever live,
And endless good diffuse, and endless praise receive.

Charity.

As through the artist's intervening glass,
Our eye observes the distant planets pass;
A little we discover; but allow,
That more remains unseen, than art can show:
So whilst our mind its knowledge would improve;
(Its feeble eye intent on things above)
High as we may, we lift our reason up,
By Faith directed, and confirmed by Hope:
Yet are we able only to survey
Dawnings of beams, and promises of day.
Heaven's fuller effluence mocks our dazzled sight;
Too great its swiftness, and too strong its light.

But soon the mediate clouds shall be dispelled:
The Sun shall soon be face to face beheld,
In all his robes, with all his glory on,
Seated sublime on his meridian throne.

Then constant Faith, and holy Hope shall die,
One lost in certainty, and one in joy:
Whilst thou, more happy power, fair Charity,
Triumphant sister, greatest of the three,
Thy office, and thy nature still the same,
Lasting thy lamp, and unconsumed thy flame,
Shalt still survive ⸺
Shalt stand before the host of heaven confest,
For ever blessing, and for ever blest.

Phineas Fletcher.

Born 1582. Died 1650.

THE SHEPHERD'S LIFE.

Thrice, oh, thrice happy shepherd's life and state,
  When courts are happiness, unhappy pawns!
His cottage low, and safely humble gate,
  Shuts out proud Fortune, with her scorns and fawns;
    No feared treason breaks his quiet sleep;
    Singing all day, his flocks he learns to keep;
Himself as innocent as are his simple sheep.

No Syrian worms he knows, that with their thread
  Draw out their silken lives:—nor silken pride:
His lambs' warm fleece well fits his little need,
  Not in that proud Sidonian tincture dyed:
    No empty hopes, no courtly fears him fright;
    No begging wants his middle fortune bite:
But sweet content exiles both misery and spite.

Instead of music and base flattering tongues,
  Which wait to first-salute my lord's uprise,
The cheerful lark wakes him with early songs,
  And birds' sweet whistling notes unlock his eyes.
    In country plays is all the strife he uses;
    Or sing, or dance unto the rural Muses;
And but in music's sports all difference refuses.

His certain life, that never can deceive him,
  Is full of thousand sweets and rich content:
The smooth-leaved beeches in the field receive him
  With coolest shades, till noontide's rage is spent:
    His life is neither tost in boisterous seas
    Of troublous world, nor lost in slothful ease;
Pleased and full blest he lives, when he his God can
    please.

His bed of wool yields safe and quiet sleeps,
  While by his side his faithful spouse hath place:
His little son into his bosom creeps,
  The lively picture of his father's face.
    Never his humble house or state torment him;
    Less he could like, if less his God had sent him;
And when he dies, green turfs, with grassy tomb,
    content him.

Beilby Porteus.

Born 1731. Died 1808.

DEATH.

LIVE, then, while Heaven, in pity, lends thee life,
And think it all too short to wash away
By penitential tears, and deep contrition,
The scarlet of thy crimes. So shalt thou find

Rest to thy soul, so unappalled shalt meet
Death when he comes, not wantonly invite
His lingering stroke. Be it thy sole concern
With innocence to live; with patience wait
The appointed hour; too soon that hour will come
Though Nature run her course. But Nature's God
If need require, by thousand various ways,
Without thy aid, can shorten that short span,
And quench the lamp of life. O, when he comes,
Roused by the cry of wickedness extreme
To Heaven ascending from some guilty land,
Now ripe for vengeance; when he comes arrayed
In all the terrors of Almighty wrath;
Forth from his bosom plucks his lingering arm,
And on the miscreants pours destruction down,
Who can abide his coming! Who can bear
His whole displeasure? In no common form
Death then appears, but, starting into size
Enormous, measures with gigantic stride
The astonished earth, and, from his looks, throws round
Unutterable horror and dismay.
All nature lends her aid.   Each element
Arms in his cause.   Ope fly the doors of Heaven;
The fountains of the deep their barriers break;
Above, below, the rival torrents pour,
And drown Creation : or in floods of fire
Descends a livid cataract, and consumes
An impious race.   Sometimes, when all seems peace,
Wakes the grim whirlwind, and with rude embrace

Sweeps nations to their grave, or in the deep
Whelms the proud wooden world; full many a youth
Floats on his watery bier, or lies unwept
On some sad desert shore. At dead of night
In sullen silence stalks forth Pestilence:
Contagion, close behind, taints all her steps
With poisonous dew; no smiting hand is seen,
No sound is heard, but soon her secret path
Is marked with desolation: heaps on heaps
Promiscuous drop. No friend, no refuge, near,
All, all, is false and treacherous around;
All that they touch, or taste, or breathe, is Death.

Earl of Roscommon.

Born 1633. Died 1684.

FROM THE DAY OF JUDGMENT.

THE last loud trumpet's wondrous sound
Shall through the rending tombs rebound,
And wake the nations under ground.

Nature and Death shall, with surprise,
Behold the pale offender rise,
And view the Judge with conscious eyes.

Then shall, with universal dread,
The sacred mystic book be read
To try the living and the dead.

The Judge ascends his awful throne;
He makes each secret sin be known;
And all with shame confess their own.

O then! what interest shall I make,
To save my last important stake,
When the most just have cause to quake?

Thou mighty, formidable King,
Thou mercy's unexhausted spring,
Some comfortable pity bring!

Forget not what my ransom cost;
Nor let my dear-bought soul be lost,
In storms of guilty terror tost.

Thou who for me didst feel such pain,
Whose precious blood the cross did stain,
Let not those agonies be vain.

Thou whom avenging powers obey,
Cancel my debt (too great to pay)
Before the sad accounting day.

Surrounded with amazing fears,

Whose load my soul with anguish bears,
I sigh, I weep: accept my tears.

Thou who wert moved with Mary's grief,
And, by absolving of the thief,
Hast given me hope, now give relief.

Reject not my unworthy prayer;
Preserve me from that dangerous snare
Which death and gaping hell prepare.

Give my exalted soul a place
Among thy chosen right-hand race,
The sons of God, and heirs of grace.

From that insatiable abyss,
Where flames devour and serpents hiss,
Promote me to thy seat of bliss.

Prostrate my contrite heart I rend,
My God, my Father, and my Friend;
Do not forsake me in my end.

Well may they curse their second breath,
Who rise to a reviving death:
Thou great Creator of mankind,
Let guilty man compassion find!

Isaac Walton.

Born 1593. Died 1683.

THE ANGLER'S WISH.

I in these flowery meads would be:
These crystal streams should solace me;
To whose harmonious bubbling noise
I with my angle would rejoice,
    Sit here, and see the turtle-dove
    Court his chaste mate to acts of love:

Or, on that bank, feel the west wind
Breathe health and plenty: please my mind,
To see sweet dewdrops kiss these flowers,
And then washed off by April showers;
    Here, hear my Kenna sing a song:
    There, see a blackbird feed her young,

Or a laverock build her nest:
Here, give my weary spirits rest,
And raise my low-pitched thoughts above
Earth, or what poor mortals love:
    Thus, free from lawsuits and the noise
    Of princes' courts, I would rejoice;

Or, with my Bryan and a book,
Loiter long days near Shawford brook;

There sit by him, and eat my meat,
There see the sun both rise and set:
There bid good morning to next day;
There meditate my time away;
  And angle on; and beg to have
  A quiet passage to a welcome grave.

John Langhorne.

Born 1735. Died 1779.

ETERNAL PROVIDENCE.

LIGHT of the world, Immortal mind;
Father of all the human kind!
Whose boundless eye, that knows no rest,
Intent on Nature's ample breast,
Explores the space of earth and skies
And sees eternal incense rise!
To thee my humble voice I raise;
Forgive, while I presume to praise.

Though thou this transient being gave,
That shortly sinks into the grave;
Yet 'twas thy goodness still to give
A being that can think and live;

In all thy works thy wisdom see,
And stretch its towering mind to thee,
To thee my humble voice I raise;
Forgive, while I presume to praise.

And still this poor contracted span,
This life, that bears the name of man,
From thee derives its vital ray,
Eternal source of life and day!
Thy bounty still the sunshine pours,
That gilds its morn and evening hours.
To thee my humble voice I raise;
Forgive, while I presume to praise.

Through error's maze, through folly's night,
The lamp of reason lends me light;
Where stern affliction waves her rod,
My heart confides in thee, my God!
When nature shrinks, oppressed with woes,
E'en then she finds in thee repose.
To thee my humble voice I raise;
Forgive, while I presume to praise.

Affliction flies, and hope returns;
Her lamp with brighter splendour burns;
Gay love, with all his smiling train,
And peace and joy are here again.
These, these, I know, 'twas thine to give;
I trusted, and, behold, I live!

To thee my humble voice I raise;
Forgive, while I presume to praise.

Oh, may I still thy favour prove!
Still grant me gratitude and love.
Let truth and virtue guard my heart;
Nor peace, nor hope, nor joy depart:
But yet, whate'er my life may be,
My heart shall still repose on thee!
To thee my humble voice I raise;
Forgive, while I presume to praise.

James Merrick.
Born 1720. Died 1769.

THE PROVIDENCE OF GOD.

Placed on the verge of youth, my mind
    Life's opening scene surveyed;
I viewed its ills of various kind,
    Afflicted and afraid.

But chief my fear the dangers moved,
    That Virtue's path enclose:
My heart the wise pursuit approved,
    But oh! what toils oppose,

For see! ah see! while yet her ways
    With doubtful step I tread,
A hostile world its terrors raise,
    Its snares delusive spread.

Oh! how shall I, with heart prepared,
    Those terrors learn to meet?
How from the thousand snares to guard
    My inexperienced feet?

As thus I mused, oppressive sleep
    Soft o'er my temples drew
Oblivious veil.—The watery deep,
    An object strange and new,

Before me rose: on the wide shore
    Observant as I stood,
The gathering storms around me roar,
    And heave the boiling flood.

Near, and more near, the billows rise,
    E'en now my steps they lave;
And death to my affrighted eyes
    Approached in every wave.

What hope, or whither to retreat,
    Each nerve at once unstrung;
Chill fear had fettered fast my feet,
    And chained my speechless tongue

The Providence of God.

I feel my heart within me die;
   When sudden to mine ear
A voice descending from on high
   Reproved my erring fear:

" What though the swelling surge thou see,
   Impatient to devour,
Rest, mortal, rest on God's decree,
   And thankful own his power.

" Know when he made the deep appear,
   'Thus far,' the Almighty said—
'Thus far, nor farther, rage, and here
   Let thy proud waves be stayed.'"

I heard, and lo! at once controlled,
   The waves in wild retreat,
Back on themselves reluctant rolled,
   And murmuring left my feet.

Deeps to assembling deeps in vain
   Once more the signal gave
The shores the rushing weight sustain,
   And check the usurping wave.

Convinced in nature's volume wise,
   The imaged truth I read,
And sudden from my waking eyes
   The instructive vision fled.

Then why thus heavy, O my soul!
    Say, why distrustful still,
Thy thoughts with vain impatience roll,
    O'er scenes of future ill?

Let faith suppress each rising fear,
    Each anxious doubt exclude;
Thy Maker's will has placed thee here,
    A Maker wise and good.

He to thy every trial knows
    Its just restraint to give;
Attentive to behold thy woes,
    And faithful to relieve.

Then why thus heavy, O my soul!
    Say, why distrustful still,
Thy thoughts with vain impatience roll
    O'er scenes of future ill?

Though griefs unnumbered throng thee round
    Still in thy God confide,
Whose finger marks the seas their bound,
    And curbs the headlong tide.

Reginald Heber.

Born 1783.   Died 1826.

EARLY PIETY.

By cool Siloam's shady rill
 How sweet the lily grows!
How sweet the breath beneath the hill
 Of Sharon's dewy rose!

Lo! such the child whose early feet
 The paths of peace have trod;
Whose secret heart, with influence sweet,
 Is upward drawn to God!

By cool Siloam's shady rill
 The lily must decay;
The rose that blooms beneath the hill
 Must shortly fade away.

And soon, too soon, the wintry hour
 Of man's maturer age
Will shake the soul with sorrow's power,
 And stormy passion's rage!

O Thou, whose infant feet were found
 Within Thy Father's shrine!

Whose years, with changeless virtue crowned,
  Were all alike Divine;

Dependent on Thy bounteous breath,
  We seek Thy grace alone,
In childhood, manhood, age, and death,
  To keep us still Thine own!

John Pomfret.

Born 1677. Died 1703.

LINES TO A FRIEND WISHFUL TO BE MARRIED.

I WOULD not have you choose a mate,
From too exalted, or too mean a state;
For in both these we may expect to find
A creeping spirit, or a haughty mind.
Who moves within the middle region, shares
The least disquiets, and the smallest cares.
Let her extraction with true lustre shine;
If something brighter, not too bright for thine:
Her education liberal, not great;
Neither inferior nor above her state.
Let her have wit; but let that wit be free
From affectation, pride, or pedantry:

For the effect of woman's wit is such,
Too little is as dangerous as too much.
But chiefly let her humour close with thine ;
Unless where your's does to a fault incline ;
The least disparity in this destroys,
Like sulphurous blasts, the very buds of joys.
Her person amiable, straight, and free
From natural, or chance deformity.
Let not her years exceed, if equal thine ;
For women past their vigour, soon decline :
Her fortune competent ; and, if thy sight
Can reach so far, take care 'tis gathered right.
If thine's enough, then her's may be the less :
Do not aspire to riches in excess.
For that which makes our lives delightful prove,
Is a genteel sufficiency and love.

Tobias Smollett.

Born 1721. Died 1771.

THE TEARS OF SCOTLAND.

WRITTEN IN THE YEAR 1746.

MOURN, hapless Caledonia, mourn
Thy banished peace—thy laurels torn !
Thy sons, for valour long renowned,
Lie slaughtered on their native ground ;

Thy hospitable roofs no more
Invite the stranger to the door;
In smoky ruins sunk they lie,
The monuments of cruelty.

The wretched owner sees afar
His all become the prey of war;
Bethinks him of his babes and wife,
Then smites his breast, and curses life!
Thy swains are famished on the rocks
Where once they fed their wanton flocks:
Thy ravished virgins shriek in vain;
Thy infants perish on the plain.

What boots it then, in every clime
Through the wide-spreading waste of time,
Thy martial glory, crowned with praise,
Still shone with undiminished blaze?
Thy towering spirit now is broke,
Thy neck is bended to the yoke.
What foreign arms could never quell,
By civil rage and rancour fell.

The rural pipe and merry lay
No more shall cheer the happy day:
No social scenes of gay delight
Beguile the dreary winter night;
No strains, but those of sorrow flow,
And nought be heard but sounds of woe,

While the pale phantoms of the slain
Glide nightly o'er the silent plain.

O baneful cause! oh fatal morn,
Accursed to ages yet unborn!
The sons against their fathers stood,
The parent shed his children's blood.
Yet, when the rage of battle ceased,
The victor's soul was not appeased;
The naked and forlorn must feel
Devouring flames, and murdering steel!

The pious mother, doomed to death,
Forsaken, wanders o'er the heath;
The bleak wind whistles round her head,
Her helpless orphans cry for bread;
Bereft of shelter, food, and friend,
She views the shades of night descend,
And stretched beneath the inclement skies,
Weeps o'er her tender babes, and dies.

While the warm blood bedews my veins,
And unimpaired remembrance reigns,
Resentment of my country's fate
Within my filial breast shall beat;
And, spite of her insulting foe,
My sympathizing verse shall flow:—
"Mourn, hapless Caledonia! mourn
Thy banished peace, thy laurels torn!"

William Mason.

Born 1725. Died 1797.

ODE TO TRUTH.

FROM ELFRIDA.

Say, will no white-robed Son of Light,
Swift-darting from his heavenly height,
  Here deign to take his hallowed stand;
  Here wave his amber locks; unfold
  His pinions clothed with downy gold;
Here smiling stretch his tutelary wand?
And you, ye host of Saints, for ye have known
Each dreary path in Life's perplexing maze,
  Though now ye circle yon eternal throne
  With harpings high of inexpressive praise,
  Will not your train descend in radiant state,
To break with Mercy's beam this gathering cloud of Fate?

'Tis silence all. No son of light
Darts swiftly from his heavenly height;
  No train of radiant saints descend,
  "Mortals, in vain ye hope to find,
  If guilt, if fraud, has stained your mind,
Or Saint to hear, or Angel to defend."

Ode to Truth.

So Truth proclaims. I hear the sacred sound
Burst from the centre of her burning throne:
   Where aye she sits with star-wreathed lustre
     crowned:
A bright Sun clasps her adamantine zone.
   So Truth proclaims: her awful voice I hear:
With many a solemn pause it slowly meets my ear.

   "Attend, ye Sons of Men; attend, and say,"
Does not enough of my refulgent ray
   Break through the veil of your mortality!
   Say, does not reason in this form descry
Unnumbered, nameless glories, that surpass
The Angel's floating pomp, the Seraph's glowing grace?

   Shall then your earth-born daughters vie
   With me? Shall she, whose brightest eye
     But emulates the diamond's blaze,
   Whose cheek but mocks the peach's bloom,
   Whose breath the hyacinth's perfume,
Whose melting voice the warbling woodlark's lays,
   Shall she be deemed my rival? Shall a form
Of elemental dross, of mouldering clay,
   Vie with these charms imperial? The poor worm
Shall prove her contest vain. Life's little day
   Shall pass, and she is gone: while I appear
Flushed with the bloom of youth through Heaven's
     eternal year.

Know, Mortals, know, ere first ye sprung,
Ere first these orbs in æther hung,
 I shone amid the heavenly throng.
These eyes beheld Creation's day,
This voice began the choral lay,
And taught Archangels their triumphant song.
 'Pleased I surveyed bright Nature's gradual birth,
Saw infant Light with kindling lustre spread,
 Soft vernal fragrance clothe the flowering earth,
And Ocean heave on his extended bed ;
 Saw the tall pine aspiring pierce the sky,
The tawny Lion stalk, the rapid Eagle fly.

Last, Man arose, erect in youthful grace,
Heaven's hallowed image stampt upon his face,
 And, as he rose, the high behest was given.
 "That I alone of all the host of heaven,
Should reign Protectress of the godlike Youth."
Thus the Almighty spake ; he spake and called me
 Truth.

Sir Walter Raleigh.
Born 1552. Died 1618.

THE SILENT LOVER.

Passions are likened best to floods and streams,
The shallow murmur, but the deep are dumb;
So when affection yields discourse, it seems
The bottom is but shallow whence they come;
They that are rich in words must needs discover
They are but poor in that which makes a lover.

    Wrong not, sweet mistress of my heart,
      The merit of true passion,
    With thinking that he feels no smart
      That sues for no compassion.

    Since if my plaints were not to approve
      The conquest of thy beauty,
    It comes not from defect of love,
      But fear to exceed my duty.

    For not knowing that I sue to serve
      A saint of such perfection
    As all desire, but none deserve
      A place in her affection,

I rather choose to want relief
Than venture the revealing;
Where glory recommends the grief,
Despair disdains the healing.

Silence in love betrays more woe
Than words, though ne'er so witty;
A beggar that is dumb, you know,
May challenge double pity.

Then wrong not, dearest to my heart,
My love for secret passion;
He smarteth most who hides his smart,
And sues for no compassion.

Thomas Penrose.

Born 1743. Died 1779.

THE FIELD OF BATTLE.

Faintly brayed the battle's roar
    Distant down the hollow wind;
Panting terror fled before,
    Wounds and death were left behind.

The war-fiend cursed the sunken day,
　　That checked his fierce pursuit too soon ;
While, scarcely lighting to the prey,
　　Low hung, and lowered the bloody moon.

The field, so late the hero's pride,
　　Was now with various carnage spread ;
And floated with a crimson tide,
　　That drenched the dying and the dead.

O'er the sad scene of dreariest view,
　　Abandoned all to horrors wild,
With frantic step Maria flew,
　　Maria, sorrow's early child ;

By duty led, for every vein
　　Was warmed by Hymen's purest flame ;
With Edgar o'er the wint'ry main
　　She, lovely, faithful wanderer, came.

For well she thought, a friend so dear
　　In darkest hours might joy impart ;
Her warrior, faint with toil, might cheer,
　　Or soothe her bleeding warrior's smart.

Though looked for long—in chill affright,
　　(The torrent bursting from her eye)
She heard the signal for the fight—
　　While her soul trembled in a sigh—

She heard, and clasped him to her breast,
  Yet scarce could urge the inglorious stay;
His manly heart the charm confest—
  Then broke the charm,—and rushed away.

Too soon in few—but deadly words,
  Some flying straggler breathed to tell,
That in the foremost strife of swords
  The young, the gallant Edgar fell.

She prest to hear—she caught the tale—
  At every sound her blood congealed;—
With terror bold—with terror pale,
  She sprung to search the fatal field.

O'er the sad scene in dire amaze
  She went—with courage not her own—
On many a corpse she cast her gaze—
  And turned her ear to many a groan.

Drear anguish urgèd her to press
  Full many a hand, as wild she mourned;—
—Of comfort glad, the drear caress,
  The damp, chill, dying hand returned.

Her ghastly hope was well nigh fled—
  When late pale Edgar's form she found,
Half-buried with the hostile dead,
  And gored with many a grisly wound.

She knew—she sunk—the night-bird screamed,
  —The moon withdrew her troubled light,
And left the fair,—though fallen she seemed—
  To worse than death—and deepest night.

Colley Cibber.
Born 1671. Died 1757.

THE BLIND BOY.

O SAY! what is that thing called light,
  Which I must ne'er enjoy?
What are the blessings of the sight?
  O tell your poor blind boy!

You talk of wondrous things you see,
  You say the sun shines bright;
I feel him warm, but how can he
  Or make it day or night.

My day or night myself I make,
  Whene'er I sleep or play;
And could I ever keep awake,
  With me 't were always day.

With heavy sighs I often hear
  You mourn my hapless woe;

But sure with patience I can bear
A loss I ne'er can know.

Then let not what I cannot have
My cheer of mind destroy;
Whilst thus I sing, I am a king,
Although a poor blind boy.

John Dryden.

Born 1631.   Died 1700.

ALEXANDER'S FEAST, OR, THE POWER OF MUSIC.

'Twas at the royal feast for Persia won
By Philip's warlike son—
Aloft in awful state
The godlike hero sate
On his imperial throne;
His valiant peers were placed around,
Their brows with roses and with myrtles bound
(So should desert in arms be crowned);
The lovely Thais by his side
Sate like a blooming eastern bride
In flower of youth and beauty's pride:—
Happy, happy, happy pair!

Alexander's Feast.

None but the brave
None but the brave
None but the brave deserves the fair!

  Timotheus placed on high
Amid the tuneful quire
With flying fingers touched the lyre:
The trembling notes ascend the sky
And heavenly joys inspire.
The song began from Jove
Who left his blissful seats above—
Such is the power of mighty love!
A dragon's fiery form belied the god;
Sublime on radiant spires he rode
When he to fair Olympia prest,
And while he sought her snowy breast;
Then round her slender waist he curled,
And stamped an image of himself, a sovereign
    of the world.
—The listening crowd admire the lofty sound!
A present deity! they shout around:
A present deity! the vaulted roofs rebound!
With ravished ears
The monarch hears,
Assumes the god;
Affects to nod
And seems to shake the spheres.

  The praise of Bacchus then the sweet musician
    sung:

Of Bacchus ever fair and ever young:
The jolly god in triumph comes!
Sound the trumpets, beat the drums!
Flushed with a purple grace
He shows his honest face:
Now give the hautboys breath; he comes, he comes!
Bacchus, ever fair and young,
Drinking joys did first ordain;
Bacchus' blessings are a treasure,
Drinking is the soldier's pleasure:
Rich the treasure
Sweet the pleasure,
Sweet is pleasure after pain.

    Soothed with the sound, the king grew vain;
Fought all his battles o'er again,
And thrice he routed all his foes, and thrice he
    slew the slain!
The master saw the madness rise,
His glowing cheeks, his ardent eyes;
And while he heaven and earth defied
Changed his hand and checked his pride.
He chose a mournful muse
Soft pity to infuse:
He sung Darius great and good,
By too severe a fate
Fallen, fallen, fallen, fallen,
Fallen from his high estate,
And weltering in his blood;

Deserted, at his utmost need,
By those his former bounty fed;
On the bare earth exposed he lies
With not a friend to close his eyes.
—With downcast looks the joyless victor sate,
Revolving in his altered soul
The various turns of chance below;
And now and then a sigh he stole,
And tears began to flow.

The mighty master smiled to see
That love was in the next degree;
'Twas but a kindred sound to move,
For pity melts the mind to love.
Softly sweet, in Lydian measures
Soon he soothed his soul to pleasures.
War, he sung, is toil and trouble,
Honour but an empty bubble,
Never ending, still beginning;
Fighting still, and still destroying;
If the world be worth thy winning,
Think, O think, it worth enjoying:
Lovely Thais sits beside thee,
Take the good the gods provide thee!
—The many rend the skies with loud applause;
So Love was crowned, but Music won the cause.
The prince, unable to conceal his pain,
Gazed on the fair
Who caused his care,

And sighed and looked, sighed and looked,
Sighed and looked, and sighed again:
At length with love and wine at once opprest
The vanquished victor sunk upon her breast.

Now strike the golden lyre again:
A louder yet, and yet a louder strain!
Break his bands of sleep asunder
And rouse him like a rattling peal of thunder.
Hark, hark! the horrid sound
Has raised up his head:
As awaked from the dead
And amazed he stares around.
Revenge, revenge, Timotheus cries,
See the Furies arise!
See the snakes that they rear
How they hiss in their hair,
And the sparkles that flash from their eyes!
Behold a ghastly band
Each a torch in his hand!
Those are Grecian ghosts, that in battle were slain
And unburied remain
Inglorious on the plain:
Give the vengeance due
To the valiant crew!
Behold how they toss their torches on high,
How they point to the Persian abodes
And glittering temples of their hostile gods.
—The princes applaud with a furious joy:

And the king seized a flambeau with zeal to destroy;
Thais led the way
To light him to his prey,
And like another Helen, fired another Troy!

—Thus, long ago,
Ere heaving bellows learned to blow,
While organs yet were mute,
Timotheus, to his breathing flute
And sounding lyre
Could swell the soul to rage, or kindle soft desire.
At last divine Cecilia came,
Inventress of the vocal frame;
The sweet enthusiast from her sacred store
Enlarged the former narrow bounds,
And added length to solemn sounds,
With Nature's mother-wit, and arts unknown before.
—Let old Timotheus yield the prize
Or both divide the crown;
He raised a mortal to the skies;
She drew an angel down!

George Wither.

Born 1588. Died 1669.

THE SHEPHERD'S RESOLUTION.

SHALL I, wasting in despair,
Die because a woman's fair?
Or my cheeks make pale with care
'Cause another's rosy are?
Be she fairer than the day
Or the flowery meads in May—
    If she be not so to me
    What care I how fair she be?

Shall my foolish heart be pined
'Cause I see a woman kind;
Or a well disposèd nature
Joinèd with a lovely feature?
Be she meeker, kinder, than
Turtle-dove or pelican,
    If she be not so to me
    What care I how kind she be?

Shall a woman's virtues move
Me to perish for her love?
Or her merit's value known
Make me quite forget mine own?

The Shepherd's Resolution.

Be she with that goodness blest
Which may gain her name of Best;
   If she seem not such to me,
   What care I how good she be?

'Cause her fortune seems too high,
Shall I play the fool and die?
Those that bear a noble mind
Where they want of riches find,
Think what with them they would do
Who without them dare to woo;
   And unless that mind I see,
   What care I though great she be?

Great or good, or kind or fair,
I will ne'er the more despair;
If she love me, this believe,
I will die ere she shall grieve;
If she slight me when I woo,
I can scorn and let her go;
   For if she be not for me,
   What care I for whom she be?

John Leyden.

Born 1775. Died 1811.

TO THE EVENING STAR.

How sweet thy modest light to view,
 Fair Star, to love and lovers dear!
While trembling on the falling dew,
 Like beauty shining through a tear.

Or, hanging o'er that mirror-stream,
 To mark that image trembling there,
Thou seem'st to smile with softer gleam,
 To see thy lovely face so fair.

Though, blazing o'er the arch of night,
 The moon thy timid beams outshine,
As far as thine each starry light;—
 Her rays can never vie with thine.

Thine are the soft enchanting hours,
 When twilight lingers on the plain,
And whispers to the closing flowers
 That soon the sun will rise again.

Thine is the breeze that, murmuring bland
 As music, wafts the lover's sigh,

And bids the yielding heart expand
  In love's delicious ecstasy.

Fair Star! though I be doomed to prove
  That rapture's tears are mixed with pain,
Ah, still I feel 'tis sweet to love!
  But sweeter to be loved again.

Allan Cunningham.

Born 1784. Died 1842.

A WET SHEET AND A FLOWING SEA.

A wet sheet and a flowing sea,
  A wind that follows fast,
And fills the white and rustling sail,
  And bends the gallant mast;
And bends the gallant mast, my boys,
  While, like the eagle free,
Away the good ship flies, and leaves
  Old England on the lea.

O for a soft and gentle wind!
  I heard a fair one cry;
But give to me the snoring breeze,
  And white waves heaving high;

And white waves heaving high, my boys,
    The good ship tight and free—
The world of waters is our home,
    And merry men are we.

There's tempest in yon hornèd moon,
    And lightning in yon cloud;
But hark, the music, mariners!
    The wind is piping loud;
The wind is piping loud, my boys,
    The lightning flashing free—
While the hollow oak our palace is,
    Our heritage the sea.

Joanna Baillie.

Born 1762. Died 1851.

THE NEW YEAR'S GIFT.

ALL white hung the bushes o'er Elaw's sweet stream,
And pale from its banks the long icicles gleam;
The first peep of morning just peers through the sky,
And here, at thy door, gentle Mary, am I.

With the dawn of the year, and the dawn of the light,
The one that best loves thee stands first in thy sight;

Then welcomed, dear maid, with my gift let me be,
A ribbon, a kiss, and a blessing for thee!

Last year, of earth's treasures I gave thee my part,
The new year before it I gave thee my heart;
And now, gentle Mary, I greet thee again,
When only this hand and a blessing remain!

Though time should run on with his sack full of care,
And wrinkle thy cheek, maid, and whiten thy hair,
Yet still on this morn shall my offering be,
A ribbon, a kiss, and a blessing for thee!

Alexander Wilson.

Born 1766. Died 1813.

THE AMERICAN BLUE-BIRD.

When winter's cold tempests and snows are no more,
    Green meadows and brown-furrowed fields re-appear-
       ing,
The fishermen hauling their shad to the shore,
    And cloud-cleaving geese to the lakes are a-steering,
When first the lone butterfly flits on the wing;
    When red grow the maples, so fresh and so pleasing,

O then comes the Blue-bird, the herald of spring!
   And hails with his warblings the charms of the
      season.

Then loud piping frogs make the marshes to ring;
   Then warm glows the sunshine, and fine is the
      weather;
The blue woodland flowers just beginning to spring,
   And spicewood and sassafras budding together;
O then to your gardens, ye housewives, repair!
   Your walks border up; sow and plant at your leisure;
The Blue-bird will chaunt from his box such an air,
   That all your hard toils will seem truly a pleasure.

He flits through the orchard, he visits each tree,
   The red flowering peach and the apples' sweet
      blossoms;
He snaps up destroyers wherever they be,
   And seizes the caitiffs that lurk in their bosoms;
He drags the vile grub from the corn it devours,
   The worms from their webs, where they riot and
      welter;
His song and his services freely are ours,
   And all that he asks is in summer a shelter.

The ploughman is pleased when he gleans in his train,
   Now searching the furrows,—now mounting to
      cheer him;
The gardener delights in his sweet simple strain,

And leans on his spade to survey and to hear him;
The slow lingering school-boys forget they'll be chid,
   While gazing intent as he warbles before 'em,
In mantle of sky-blue, and bosom so red,
   That each little loiterer seems to adore him.

When all the gay scenes of the summer are o'er,
   And autumn slow enters, so silent and sallow,
And millions of warblers, that charmed us before,
   Have fled in the train of the sun-seeking swallow;
The Blue-bird, forsaken, yet true to his home,
   Still lingers, and looks for a milder to-morrow,
Till forced by the horrors of winter to roam,
   He sings his adieu in a lone note of sorrow.

While spring's lovely season, serene, dewy, warm,
   The green face of earth, and the pure blue of heaven,
Or love's native music have influence to charm,
   Or sympathy's glow to our feelings are given;
Still dear to each bosom the Blue-bird shall be;
   His voice, like the thrillings of hope, is a treasure·
For through bleakest storms, if a calm he h
   He comes to remind us of sunshine and pleasure!

James Hogg.

Born 1782. Died 1835.

THE SKYLARK.

Bird of the wilderness,
Blithesome and cumberless,
Sweet be thy matin o'er moorland and lea!
Emblem of happiness,
Blest is thy dwelling-place—
Oh to abide in the desert with thee!
Wild is thy lay and loud,
Far in the downy cloud,
Love gives it energy, love gave it birth.
Where, on thy dewy wing,
Where art thou journeying?
Thy lay is in heaven, thy love is on earth.

O'er fell and fountain sheen,
O'er moor and mountain green,
O'er the red streamer that heralds the day,
Over the cloudlet dim,
Over the rainbow's rim,
Musical cherub, soar, singing, away!
Then, when the gloaming comes,
Low in the heather blooms,

Sweet will thy welcome and bed of love be,
    Emblem of happiness,
    Blest is thy dwelling-place—
Oh! to abide in the desert with thee!

Thomas Pringle.
Born 1789. Died 1834.

THE EMIGRANT'S FAREWELL.

Our native land—our native vale—
    A long and last adieu!
Farewell to bonny Teviotdale,
    And Cheviot mountains blue.

Farewell, ye hills of glorious deeds,
    And streams renowned in song—
Farewell ye braes and blossomed meads,
    Our hearts have loved so long.

Farewell, the blithesome broomy knowes,
    Where thyme and harebells grow—
Farewell, the hoary, haunted howes,
    O'erhung with birk and sloe.

The mossy cave and mouldering tower
    That skirt our native dell—

The martyr's grave, and lover's bower,
  We bid a sad farewell!

Home of our love! our father's home!
  Land of the brave and free!
The sail is flapping on the foam
  That bears us far from thee!

We seek a wild and distant shore,
  Beyond the western main—
We leave thee to return no more,
  Nor view thy cliffs again!

Our native land—our native vale—
  A long and last adieu!
Farewell to bonny Teviotdale,
  And Scotland's mountains blue!

Allan Ramsay.

Born 1685. Died 1758.

· LOCHABER.

Farewell to Lochaber, farewell to my Jean,
Where heartsome wi' her I ha'e mony a day been;
To Lochaber no more, to Lochaber no more,
We'll maybe return to Lochaber no more.

Lochaber.

These tears that I shed, they're a' for my dear,
And no for the dangers attending on weir;
Though borne on rough seas to a far bloody shore,
Maybe to return to Lochaber no more!

Though hurricanes rise, though rise every wind,
No tempest can equal the storm in my mind;
Though loudest of thunders on louder waves roar,
There's naething like leavin' my love on the shore.
To leave thee behind me my heart is sair pained;
But by ease that's inglorious no fame can be gained
And beauty and love's the reward of the brave;
And I maun deserve it before I can crave.

Then glory, my Jeanie, maun plead my excuse;
Since honour commands me, how can I refuse?
Without it, I ne'er can have merit for thee;
And losing thy favour I'd better not be.
I gae then, my lass, to win honour and fame;
And if I should chance to come glorious hame,
I'll bring a heart to thee with love running o'er,
And then I'll leave thee and Lochaber no more.

John Cunningham.

Born 1729. Died 1773.

KATE OF ABERDEEN.

THE silver moon's enamoured beam
    Steals softly through the night,
To wanton with the winding stream,
    And kiss reflected light.
To beds of state go, balmy sleep,
    ('Tis where you've seldom been,)
May's vigils while the shepherds keep
    With Kate of Aberdeen.

Upon the green the virgins wait,
    In rosy chaplets gay,
Till morn unbar her golden gate,
    And give the promised May.
Methinks I hear the maids declare,
    The promised May, when seen,
Not half so fragrant or so fair
    As Kate of Aberdeen.

Strike up the tabor's boldest notes,
    We'll rouse the nodding grove:
The nested birds shall raise their throats,
    And hail the maid I love:

And see the matin lark mistakes,
    He quits the tufted green;
Fond bird! 'tis not the morning breaks—
    'Tis Kate of Aberdeen.

Now lightsome o'er the level mead,
    Where midnight fairies rove,
Like them the jocund dance we'll lead,
    Or tune the reed to love;
For see the rosy May draws nigh,
    She claims a virgin queen;
And hark, the happy shepherd's cry,
    'Tis Kate of Aberdeen.

---

*Anne Hunter.**

Born 1742. Died 1821.

INDIAN DEATH SONG.

The sun sets in night, and the stars shun the day,
But glory remains when their lights fade away.
Begin, ye tormentors, your threats are in vain,
For the son of Alknomook will never complain.

* Mrs. Hunter was the wife of John Hunter, the celebrated anatomist; her maiden name was Home.

Remember the arrows he shot from his bow ;
Remember your chiefs by his hatchet laid low.
Why so slow ? Do you wait till I shrink from the
    pain ?
No ! the son of Alknomook shall never complain.

Remember the wood where in ambush we lay,
And the scalps which we bore from your nation away :
Now the flame rises fast ; ye exult in my pain ;
But the son of Alknomook can never complain.

I go to the land where my father is gone ;
His ghost shall rejoice in the fame of his son.
Death comes like a friend, to relieve me from pain ;
And thy son, O Alknomook, has scorned to complain !

Edwin Waugh.

Born 1819.

COME WHOAM TO THY CHILDER AN' ME.

Aw've just mended th' fire wi' a cob ;
  Owd Swaddle has brought thi new shoon ;
There's some nice bacon-collops o'th hob,
  An' a quart o' ale-posset i'th oon ;

Come whoam to thy Childer an' Me.

Aw've brought thi top-cwot, does ta know,
  For th' rain's comin' deawn very dree;
An' th' har'stone's as white as new snow;
  Come whoam to thi childer an' me.

When aw put little Sally to bed,
  Hoo cried, 'cose her feyther weren't theer,
So, aw kissed th' little thing, an' aw said
  Tha'ed bring her a ribbon fro th' fair;
An' aw gav her her doll, an' some rags,
  An' a nice little white cotton bo';
An' aw kissed her again; but hoo said
  At hoo wanted to kiss *thee* an' o'.

An' Dick, too, aw'd sich wark wi' him,
  Afore aw could get him up stairs;
Thae towd him thae'd bring him a drum,
  He said, when he're sayin' his prayers:
Then he looked i' my faze, an' he said,
  " Has th' boggarts taen houd o' my dad?"
An' he cried whol his e'en were quite red;—
  He likes thee some weel, does yon lad!

At th' lung-length, aw geet 'em laid still;
  An' aw hearken't folk's feet at went by;
So aw iron't o' my clooas reet weel,
  An' aw hanged 'em o'th maiden to dry;
When aw'd mended thi stockin's an' shirts,
  Aw sit deawn to knit i' my cheer,

An' aw rayley did feel rayther hurt.—
   Mon, aw'm *one-ly* when theaw artn't theer.

"Aw've a drum an' a trumpet for Dick ;
   Aw've a yard o' blue ribbin for Sal ;
Aw've a book full o' babs ; an' a stick
   An' some 'bacco an' pipes for mysel ;
Aw've brought thee some coffee an' tay ;
   Iv thae'll *feel* i' my pocket, thae'll *see* ;
An' aw've bought tho a new cap to-day,—
   But, aw olez bring summat for *thee !*

"God bless tho, mo lass ; aw'll go whoam,
   An' aw'll kiss thee an' th' childer o' reawnd ;
Thae knows, at wheerever aw roam,
   Aw'm fain to get back to th' owd greawnd ;
Aw can do wi' a crack o'er a glass ;
   Aw can do wi' a bit ov a spree ;
But aw've no gradely comfort, mo lass,
   Except wi' yon childer an' thee !"

Alexander Smith.

Born 1830.

LADY BARBARA.

EARL GAWAIN wooed the Lady Barbara,—
High-thoughted Barbara, so white and cold!
'Mong broad-branched beeches in the summer shaw,
In soft green light his passion he has told.
When rain-beat winds did shriek across the wold,
The Earl to take her fair reluctant ear
Framed passion-trembled ditties manifold;
Silent she sat his am'rous breath to hear,
With calm and steady eyes, her heart was otherwhere.

He sighed for her through all the summer weeks;
Sitting beneath a tree whose fruitful boughs
Bore glorious apples with smooth-shining cheeks,
Earl Gawain came and whispered, "Lady, rouse!
Thou art no vestal held in holy vows;
Out with our falcons to the pleasant heath."
Her father's blood leapt up unto her brows—
He who, exulting on the trumpet's breath,
Came charging like a star across the lists of death,

Trembled, and passed before her high rebuke:
And then she sat, her hands clasped round her knee:

Like one far-thoughted was the lady's look,
For in a morning cold as misery
She saw a lone ship sailing on the sea;
Before the north 't was driven like a cloud,
High on the poop a man sat mournfully:
The wind was whistling thorough mast and shroud.
And to the whistling wind thus did he sing aloud:—

"Did it look last night upon my native vales,
Thou Sun! that from the drenching sea hast clomb?
Ye demon winds! that glut my gaping sails,
Upon the salt sea must I ever roam,
Wander for ever on the barren foam?
O happy are ye, resting mariners.
O Death, that thou wouldst come and take me home!
A hand unseen this vessel onward steers,
And onward I must float through slow moon-measured
    years.

"Ye winds! when like a curse ye drove us on,
Frothing the waters, and along our way,
Nor cape nor headland through red mornings shone,
One wept aloud, one shuddered down to pray,
One howled, 'Upon the Deep we are astray.'
On our wild hearts his words fell like a blight:
In one short hour my hair was stricken gray,
For all the crew sank ghastly in my sight
As we went driving on through the cold starry
    night.

"Madness fell on me in my loneliness,
The sea foamed curses, and the reeling sky
Became a dreadful face which did oppress
Me with the weight of its unwinking eye.
It fled, when I burst forth into a cry—
A shoal of fiends came on me from the deep;
I hid, but in all corners they did pry,
And dragged me forth, and round did dance and leap;
They mouthed on me in dream, and tore me from
    sweet sleep.

"Strange constellations burned above my head,
Strange birds around the vessel shrieked and flew,
Strange shapes, like shadows, through the clear sea fled,
As our lone ship, wide-winged, came rippling through,
Angering to foam the smooth and sleeping blue."
The lady sighed, "Far, far upon the sea,
My own Sir Arthur, could I die with you!
The wind blows shrill between my love and me."
Fond heart! the space between was but the apple-tree.

There was a cry of joy, with seeking hands
She fled to him, like worn bird to her nest;
Like washing water on the figured sands,
His being came and went in sweet unrest,
As from the mighty shelter of his breast
The Lady Barbara her head uprears
With a wan smile, "Methinks I'm but half blest:
Now when I've found thee, after weary years,
I cannot see thee, love! so blind I am with tears."

Charles Mackay.

Born 1814.

THE SAILOR'S WIFE.—Part I.

I've a letter from thy sire,
   Baby mine, Baby mine!
I can read and never tire,
    Baby mine!
He is sailing o'er the sea—
He is coming back to thee,
He is coming home to me,
    Baby mine!

He's been parted from us long
   Baby mine, Baby mine!
But if hearts be true and strong,
    Baby mine!
They shall brave Misfortune's blast,
And be overpaid at last
For all pain and sorrow passed,
    Baby mine!

Oh, I long to see his face,
   Baby mine, Baby mine!
In his old accustomed place,
    Baby mine!

Like the rose of May in bloom,
Like a star amid the gloom,
Like the sunshine in the room,
   Baby mine!

Thou wilt see him and rejoice,
   Baby mine, Baby mine!
Thou wilt know him by his voice,
   Baby mine!
By his love-looks that endear,
By his laughter ringing clear,
By his eyes that know not fear,
   Baby mine!

I'm so glad—I cannot sleep,
   Baby mine, Baby mine!
I'm so happy—I could weep,
   Baby mine!
He is sailing o'er the sea,
He is coming home to me,
He is coming back to thee,
   Baby mine!

THE SAILOR'S WIFE.—Part II.

O'er the blue ocean gleaming
 She sees a distant ship,
  As small to view
  As the white sea-mew,

Whose wings in the billows dip.
"Blow favouring gales, in her answering sails!
　Blow steadily and free!
　　Rejoicing, strong,
　　Singing a song,
　　Her rigging and her spars among,
　　And waft the vessel in pride along,
　That bears my love to me."

Nearer—still nearer driving,
　The white sails grow and swell;
　　Clear to her eyes
　　The pennant flies,
　And the flag she knows so well.
"Blow favouring gales, in her answering sails!
　Waft him, oh gentle sea!
　　And still, oh heart!
　　Thy fluttering start!
　　Why throb and beat as thou wouldst part,
　　When all so happy and blessed thou art?
　He comes again to thee!"

The swift ship drops her anchor—
　A boat puts off for shore—
　　Against its prow
　　The ripples flow,
　To the music of the oar.
"And art thou here, mine own, my dear,
　Safe from the perilous sea?—

Safe, safe at home,
No more to roam!
Blow, tempests blow—my love has come;
And sprinkle the clouds with your dashing
  foam!
He shall part no more from me!"

Philip James Bailey.

Born 1816.

LOVE.

Love is the happy privilege of the mind—
Love is the reason of all living things.
A Trinity there seems of principles,
Which represent and rule created life—
The love of self, our fellows, and our God.
In all throughout one common feeling reigns:
Each doth maintain, and is maintained by the other:
All are compatible—all needful; one
To life,—to virtue one,—and one to bliss:
Which thus together make the power, the end,
And the perfection of created Being.
From these three principles doth every deed,
Desire, and will, and reasoning, good or bad, come;
To these they all determine—sum and scheme:

The three are one in centre and in round;
Wrapping the world of life as do the skies
Our world.   Hail ! air of love, by which we live!
How sweet, how fragrant! Spirit, though unseen—
Void of gross sign—is scarce a simple essence,
Immortal, immaterial, though it be.
One only simple essence liveth—God,—
Creator, uncreate.   The brutes beneath,
The angels high above us, with ourselves,
Are but compounded things of mind and form.
In all things animate is therefore cored
An elemental sameness of existence;
For God, being Love, in love created all,
As he contains the whole and penetrates.
Seraphs love God, and angels love the good:
We love each other; and these lower lives,
Which walk the earth in thousand diverse shapes,
According to their reason, love us too:
The most intelligent affect us most.
Nay, man's chief wisdom's love—the love of God.
The new religion—final, perfect, pure—
Was that of Christ and love.   His great command—
His all-sufficing precept—was't not love?
Truly to love ourselves we must love God,—
To love God we must all his creatures love,—
To love his creatures, both ourselves and Him.
Thus love is all that's wise, fair, good, and happy !

Eliza Cook.

Born 1817.

THE OLD ARM-CHAIR.

I love it, I love it; and who shall dare
To chide me for loving that old arm-chair?
I've treasured it long as a sainted prize;
I've bedewed it with tears, and embalmed it with sighs.
'Tis bound by a thousand bands to my heart;
Not a tie will break, not a link will start.
Would ye learn the spell?—a mother sat there;
And a sacred thing is that old arm-chair.

In childhood's hour I lingered near
The hallowed seat with listening ear;
And gentle words that mother would give;
To fit me to die, and teach me to live.
She told me shame would never betide,
With truth for my creed and God for my guide;
She taught me to lisp my earliest prayer;
As I knelt beside that old arm-chair.

I sat and watched her many a day,
When her eye grew dim, and her locks were gray;
And I almost worshipped her when she smiled,
And turned from her Bible, to bless her child.

Years rolled on; but the last one sped—
My idol was shattered; my earth-star fled:
I learnt how much the heart can bear,
When I saw her die in that old arm-chair.

'Tis past, 't is past, but I gaze on it now
With quivering breath and throbbing brow:
'Twas there she nursed me; 'twas there she died:
And memory flows with lava tide.
Say it is folly, and deem me weak,
While the scalding drops start down my cheek;
But I love it, I love it; and cannot tear
My soul from a mother's old arm-chair.

James Hedderwick.

Born 1814.

THE EMIGRANTS.

The daylight was dying, the twilight was dreary,
   And eerie the face of the fast-falling night;
But, closing the shutters, we made ourselves cheery
   With gas-light and fire-light and eyes glancing bright.

When, hark! came a chorus of wailing and anguish!
   We ran to the door and looked out through the dark;

Till, gazing, at length we began to distinguish
The slow-moving masts of an ocean-bound bark.

Alas! 'twas the emigrants leaving the river,
Their homes in the city, their haunts in the dell;
From kindred and friends they had parted for ever,
But their voices still blended in cries of farewell.

We saw not the eyes that their last looks were taking;
We heard but the shouts that were meant to be cheers,
But which told of the aching of hearts that were breaking,
A past of delight and a future of tears.

And long as we listened, in lulls of the night breeze,
On our ears the sad shouting in faint music fell,
Till methought it seemed lost in the roll of the white seas,
And the rocks and the winds only echoed farewell.

More bright was our home-hearth, more bright and more cosy,
As we shut out the night and its darkness once more;
But pale were the cheeks that, so radiant and rosy,
Were flushed with delight a few moments before.

So I told how the morning, all lovely and tender,
Sweet dew on the hills, and soft light on the sea,

Would follow the exiles, and float with its splendour
    To gild the far land where their homes were to be.

In the eyes of my children were gladness and gleaming:
    Their little prayer uttered, how calm was their sleep!
But I in my dreaming could hear the wind screaming,
    And fancy I heard hoarse replies from the deep.

And often, when slumber had cooled my brow's fever,
    A dream-uttered shriek of despair broke the spell;
'Twas the voice of the emigrants leaving the river,
    And startling the night with their cries of farewell.

Adelaide Anne Procter.

A DREAM.

ALL yesterday I was spinning,
    Sitting alone in the sun;
And the dream that I spun was so lengthy,
    It lasted till day was done.

I heeded not cloud or shadow
    That flitted over the hill,
Or the humming-bees, or the swallows,
    Or the trickling of the rill.

A Dream.

I took the threads for my spinning,
　All of blue summer air,
And a flickering ray of sunlight
　Was woven in here and there.

The shadows grew longer and longer,
　The evening wind passed by,
And the purple splendour of sunset
　Was flooding the western sky.

But I could not leave my spinning,
　For so fair my dream had grown,
I heeded not, hour by hour,
　How the silent day had flown.

At last the gray shadows fell round me,
　And the night came dark and chill,
And I rose and ran down the valley,
　And left it all on the hill.

I went up the hill this morning
　To the place where my spinning lay,
There was nothing but glistening dewdrops
　Remained of my dream to-day.

William O. Peabody.

HYMN OF NATURE.

God of the earth's extended plains !
   The dark green fields contented lie ;
The mountains rise like holy towers,
   Where man might commune with the sky ;
The tall cliff challenges the storm
   That lowers upon the vale below,
Where shaded fountains send their streams
   With joyous music in their flow.

God of the dark and heavy deep !
   The waves lie sleeping on the sands,
Till the fierce trumpet of the storm
   Hath summoned up their thundering bands ;
Then the white sails are dashed like foam,
   Or hurry, trembling o'er the seas,
Till, calmed by thee, the sinking gale
   Serenely breathes, Depart in peace.

God of the forest's solemn shade !
   The grandeur of the lonely tree,
That wrestles singly with the gale,
   Lifts up admiring eyes to thee ;
But more majestic far they stand,
   When, side by side, their ranks they form

To weave on high their plumes of green,
　　And fight their battles with the storm.

God of the light and viewless air!
　　Where summer breezes sweetly flow,
Or, gathering in their angry might,
　　The fierce and wintry tempests blow;
All—from the evening's plaintive sigh,
　　That hardly lifts the drooping flower,
To the wild whirlwind's midnight cry—
　　Breathe forth the language of thy power.

God of the fair and open sky!
　　How gloriously above us springs
The tented dome of heavenly blue,
　　Suspended on the rainbow's rings!
Each brilliant star that sparkles through,
　　Each gilded cloud that wanders free
In evening's purple radiance, gives
　　The beauty of its praise to thee.

God of the rolling orbs above!
　　Thy name is written clearly bright
In the warm day's unvarying blaze,
　　Or evening's golden shower of light.
For every fire that fronts the sun,
　　And every spark that walks alone
Around the utmost verge of heaven,
　　Were kindled at thy burning throne.

God of the world! the hour must come,
  And nature's self to dust return ;
Her crumbling altars must decay,
  Her incense fires shall cease to burn ;
But still her grand and lovely scenes
  Have made man's warmest praises flow ;
For hearts grow holier as they trace
  The beauty of the world below.

George Washington Doane.

SPIRIT OF SPRING.

Spirit of Spring! when the cheek is pale,
  There is health in thy balmy air,
    And peace in that brow of beaming bright,
    And joy in that eye of sunny light,
  And golden hope in that flowing hair :
Oh! that such influence e'er should fail,
    For a moment, Spirit of Spring—
Spirit of health, peace, joy, and hope, Spirit of Spring!

Yet fail it must—for it comes of earth,
And it may not shame its place of birth,
Where the best can bloom but a single day,
And the fairest is first to fade away.

But oh! there's a changeless world above,
A world of peace, and joy, and love,
  Where, gathered from the tomb,
The holy hopes that earth has crossed,
And the pious friends we loved and lost,
  Immortally shall bloom.

Who will not watch, and strive, and pray,
That his longing soul may soar away,
  On faith's untiring wing,
To join the throng of the saints in light,
In that world, for ever fair and bright,
  Of endless, cloudless Spring!

Richard Henry Dana.

Born 1787.

THE LITTLE BEACH BIRD.

Thou little bird, thou dweller by the sea,
Why takest thou its melancholy voice?
    Why with that boding cry
    O'er the waves dost thou fly?
  Oh, rather, bird, with me,
  Through the fair land rejoice!

Thy flitting form comes ghostly dim, and pale,
As driven by a beating storm at sea;
 Thy cry is weak and scared,
 As if thy mates had shared
The doom of us. Thy wail—
 What does it bring to me?

Of thousands thou, both sepulchre and pall,
Old ocean, art! A requiem on the dead,
 From out thy gloomy cells,
 A tale of mourning tells—
Tells of man's woe and fall,
 His sinless glory fled.

Then turn thee, little bird, and take thy flight
Where the complaining sea shall sadness bring
 Thy spirit never more:
 Come, quit with me the shore,
For gladness and the light,
 Where birds of summer sing.

John G. Whittier.

THE SHIP-BUILDERS.

The sky is ruddy in the east,
    The earth is gray below,
And, spectral in the river-mist,
    The ship's white timbers show.
Then let the sounds of measured stroke
    And grating saw begin;
The broad axe to the gnarlèd oak,
    The mallet to the pin!

Hark! roars the bellows, blast on blast,
    The sooty smithy jars,
And fire-sparks, rising far and fast,
    Are fading with the stars.
All day for us the smith shall stand
    Beside that flashing forge;
All day for us his heavy hand
    The groaning anvil scourge.

From far-off hills, the panting team
    For us is toiling near;
For us the raftsmen down the stream
    Their island barges steer.

Rings out for us the axe-man's stroke
　　In forests old and still—
For us the century-circled oak
　　Falls crashing down his hill.

Up! up! in nobler toils than ours
　　No craftsmen bear a part;
We make of nature's giant powers
　　The slaves of human art.
Lay rib to rib and beam to beam,
　　And drive the treenails free;
Nor faithless joint nor yawning seam
　　Shall tempt the searching sea!

Where'er the keel of our good ship
　　The sea's rough field shall plough—
Where'er her tossing spars shall drip
　　With salt spray caught below—
That ship must heed her master's beck,
　　Her helm obey his hand,
And seamen tread her reeling deck
　　As if they trod the land.

Her oaken ribs the vulture-beak
　　Of Northern ice may peel;
The sunken rock and coral peak
　　May grate along her keel;
And know we well the painted shell
　　We give to wind and wave

The Ship-Builders.

Must float, the sailor's citadel,
   Or sink, the sailor's grave!

Ho! strike away the bars and blocks,
   And set the good ship free!
Why lingers on these dusty rocks
   The young bride of the sea?
Look! how she moves adown the grooves,
   In graceful beauty now!
How lowly on the breast she loves
   Sinks down her virgin prow!

God bless her! wheresoe'er the breeze
   Her snowy wing shall fan,
Aside the frozen Hebrides,
   Or sultry Hindostan!
Where'er in mart or in the main,
   With peaceful flag unfurled,
She helps to wind the silken chain
   Of commerce round the world!

Speed on the ship! but let her bear
   No merchandise of sin,
No groaning cargo of despair
   Her roomy hold within.
No Lethean drug for eastern lands,
   Nor poison-draught for ours;
But honest fruits of toiling hands
   And nature's sun and showers!

Be hers the prairie's golden grain,
  The desert's golden sand,
The clustered fruits of sunny Spain,
  The spice of morning-land!
Her pathway on the open main
  May blessings follow free,
And glad hearts welcome back again
  Her white sails from the sea!

Nathaniel Parker Willis.

Born 1807.

ON A PICTURE OF A GIRL,

LEADING HER BLIND MOTHER THROUGH A WOOD.

  THE green leaves as we pass
Lay their light fingers on thee unaware,
And by thy side the hazels cluster fair,
  And the low forest grass
Grows green and silken where the wood-paths wind—
Alas! for thee, sweet mother! thou art blind!

  And nature is all bright;
And the faint gray and crimson of the dawn,
Like folded curtains from the day are drawn;
  And evening's purple light

Quivers in tremulous softness on the sky—
Alas! sweet mother! for thy clouded eye!

 The moon's new silver shell
Trembles above thee, and the stars float up,
In the blue air, and the rich tulip's cup
 Is pencilled passing well,
And the swift birds on glorious pinions flee—
Alas! sweet mother! that thou canst not see!

 And the kind looks of friends
Peruse the sad expression in thy face,
And the child stops amid his bounding race,
 And the tall stripling bends
Low to thine ear with duty unforgot—
Alas! sweet mother! that thou seest them not!

 But thou canst *hear!* and love
May richly in a human tone be poured,
And the least cadence of a whispered word
 A daughter's love may prove—
And while I speak thou knowest if I smile,
Albeit thou canst not see my face the while.

 Yes, thou canst hear! and He
Who on thy sightless eye its darkness hung,
To the attentive ear, like harps, hath strung
 Heaven and earth and sea!
And 'tis a lesson in our hearts to know—
With but one sense the soul may overflow.

Mrs. L. H. Sigourney.

THE RETURN OF NAPOLEON FROM ST. HELENA.

Ho! City of the gay!
  Paris! what festal rite
Doth call thy thronging millions forth,
  All eager for the sight?
Thy soldiers line the streets
  In fixed and stern array,
With buckled helm and bayonet,
  As on the battle-day.

By square, and fountain side,
  Heads in dense masses rise,
And tower, and battlement, and tree,
  Are studded thick with eyes.
Comes there some conqueror home
  In triumph from the fight,
With spoil and captives in his train,
  The trophies of his might?

The "Arc de Triomphe" glows!
  A martial host are nigh,
France pours in long succession forth
  Her pomp of chivalry.

No clarion marks their way,
  No victor trump is blown;
Why march they on so silently,
  Told by their tread alone?

Behold! in glittering show,
  A gorgeous car of state!
The white-plumed steeds, in cloth of gold,
  Bow down beneath its weight;
And the noble warhorse, led
  Caparisoned along,
Seems fiercely for his lord to ask,
  As his red eye scans the throng.

Who rideth on yon car?
  The incense flameth high,—
Comes there some demi-god of old?
  No answer!—No reply!
Who rideth on yon car?—
  No shout his minions raise,
But by a lofty chapel dome
  The muffled hero stays.

A king is standing there,
  And with uncovered head
Receives him in the name of France:
  Receiveth whom?—*The dead!*
Was he not buried deep
  In island-cavern drear;

Girt by the sounding ocean surge?
How came that sleeper here?

Was there no rest for him
  Beneath a peaceful pall,
That thus he brake his stony tomb,
  Ere the strong angel's call?
Hark! hark! the requiem swells,
  A deep, soul-thrilling strain!
An echo, never to be heard
  By mortal ear again.

A requiem for the chief,
  Whose fiat millions slew,
The soaring eagle of the Alps,
  The crushed at Waterloo:—
The banished who returned,
  The dead who rose again,
And rode in his shroud the billows proud
  To the sunny banks of Seine.

They laid him there in state,
  That warrior strong and bold,
The imperial crown, with jewels bright,
  Upon his ashes cold,
While round those columns proud
  The blazoned banners wave,
That on a hundred fields he won,
  With the heart's blood of the brave;

And sternly there kept guard
    His veterans scarred and old,
Whose wounds of Lodi's cleaving bridge
    Or purple Leipsic told.
Yes, there, with arms reversed,
    Slow pacing, night and day,
Close watch beside the coffin kept
    Those veterans grim and gray.

A cloud is on their brow,—
    Is it sorrow for the dead?
Or memory of the fearful strife
    Where their country's legions fled?
Of Borodino's blood?
    Of Beresina's wail?
The horrors of that dire retreat,
    Which turned old History pale?

A cloud is on their brow,—
    Is it sorrow for the dead?
Or a shuddering at the wintry shaft
    By Russian tempests sped?
Where countless mounds of snow
    Marked the poor conscripts' grave,
And, pierced by frost and famine, sank
    The bravest of the brave.*

---

* An allusion to the disastrous retreat from Moscow, in which dreadful march the flower of the invading army of Napoleon was sacrificed.

A thousand trembling lamps
  The gathered darkness mock,
And velvet drapes his hearse, who died
  On bare Helena's rock;
And from the altar near,
  A never-ceasing hymn
Is lifted by the chanting priests
  Beside the taper dim.

Mysterious one, and proud!
  In the land where shadows reign,
Hast thou met the flocking ghosts of those
  Who at thy nod were slain?
Oh, when the cry of that spectral host
  Like a rushing blast shall be,
What will thine answer be to them?
  And what thy God's to thee?

INDEX.

ADDISON, On the death of, Thomas Tickell, 144.
Alexander's Feast, John Dryden, 264.
Alonzo the Brave, Matthew Gregory Lewis, 170.
Althea, To, Richard Lovelace, 203.
American Blue Bird, Alexander Wilson, 275.
Angler's Wish, The, Isaac Walton, 244.
Approach of Summer, Thomas Warton, 159.
Aurora, Ode to, Thomas Blacklock, 165.

BATTLE, The field of, Thomas Penrose, 160.
Black-Eyed Susan, John Gay, 230.
Blind Boy, Colley Cibber, 263.
Boadicea, William Cowper, 114.
Braes of Yarrow, John Logan, 130.
Burial March of Dundee, Professor Aytoun, 31.
Burial of Sir John Moore, Rev. Charles Wolfe, 56.
Byron, Genius of, Robert Pollok, 190.

CARA WAPPY, David Macbeth Moir, 4.
Celia, Song to, Ben Jonson, 113.
Charity, Matthew Prior, 235.
Charity, William Drummond, 176.
City Shower, Description of, Jonathan Swift, 209.
Clifton Grove (extract from), H. Kirke White, 87.
Come whoam to thy Childer an' me, Edwin Waugh, 284.
Conscience, Robert Southwell, 198.

Contentment, Hymn to, Thomas Parnell, 206.
Cotter's Saturday Night, Robert Burns, 121.
Cupid and Campaspe, John Lyly, 237.
Cymbeline, Dirge in, William Shakspere, 108.

DAFFODILS, Robert Herrick, 178.
Damsel of Peru, William Cullen Bryant, 58.
Danish Sea-King, Song of, William Motherwell, 134.
Day of Judgment (extract from), Earl of Roscommon, 242.
Death, Beilby Porteus, 239.
Death (extract from The Grave), Robert Blair, 155.
Death's Final Conquest, James Shirley, 175.
Delights of Virtue, Robert Ferguson, 181.
Deserted Village (extract from), Oliver Goldsmith, 69.
Disappointment, William Shenstone, 146.
Dream, A, Adelaide Anne Procter, 298.

EARLY PIETY, Reginald Heber, 251.
Early Rising and Devotion, Henry Vaughan, 204.
Earth and Heaven, Isaac Watts, 221.
Elegy Written in a Country Churchyard, Thomas Gray, 77.
Elegy Written in Spring, Michael Bruce, 186.
Emigrant's Farewell, Thomas Pringle, 279.

Index

Emigrants, The, James Hedderwick, 296.
Eternal Providence, John Langhorne, 245.
Evening Hymn, Thomas Ken, 184.
Evening Star, To the, John Leyden, 272.

Fireside, The, Nathaniel Cotton, 162.
Firmament, The, William Hubington, 233.
Flodden, Battle of (extract from Marmion), Sir Walter Scott, 62.
Flower, The, George Herbert, 212.
Forlorn, The, James Russell Lowell, 224.

GRONGAR HILL (extract from), John Dyer, 146.

HAPPY LIFE, description of, Sir Henry Wotton, 191.
Hermit, The, James Beattie, 119.
Hohenlinden, Thomas Campbell, 67.
Holy Cottage, Thomas Aird, 42.
Hymn, Joseph Addison, 139.
Hymn of Nature, William O. Peabody, 300.

Immortality of the Soul, Sir John Davis, 193.
Indian Death Song, Anne Hunter, 281.
Ivry, Lord Macaulay, 10.

JESSAMINE TREE, To a, Earl of Carlisle, 189.
Jessie the Flower o' Dumblane, Robert Tannahill, 129.

KATE of Aberdeen, John Cunningham, 282.

LADY BARBARA, Alexander Smith, 287.
Lalla Rookh (extract from), Thomas Moore, 95.
Last Day (extract from), Rev. Edward Young, 93.
Last Days of Queen Elizabeth (extract from), Sir E. Bulwer Lytton, 15.
Life, Shortness of, Abraham Cowley, 222.
Lines to a friend wishful to be married, John Pomfret, 251.
Little Beach Bird, The, Richard Henry Dana, 302.

Lochaber, Allan Ramsay, 280.
Love, Philip James Bailey, 223.
Love, Samuel Taylor Coleridge, 87.

MARGUERITE of France, Felicia Dorothea Hemans, 39.
Mariner's Wife, The, William Julius Mickle, 222.
May Queen, the, Alfred Tennyson, 1.
Miser's Mansion, The, Robert Southey, 97.
Mother's Love, James Montgomery, 195.
My Brother's Grave (extract from), Rev. John Moultrie, 21.

NEW YEAR'S GIFT, The, Joanna Baillie, 274.
Nightingale, The, Mark Akenside, 150.
Nymph's Complaint for the Death of her Fawn (extract from), Andrew Marvell, 222.

OCEAN SCENE (extract from the Shipwreck), William Falconer, 217.
Old Arm Chair, Eliza Cook, 293.

PAINS and Sorrows caused by Love, Sir Thomas Wyatt, 198.
Passions, The, William Collins, 72.
Picture of a Girl, On a, Nathaniel Parker Willis, 108.
Procession of the Seasons (extract from The Faerie Queene), Edmund Spenser, 215.
Providence of God, James Merrick, 247.

RAVEN, The, Edgar Allan Poe, 44.
Resignation, Thomas Chatterton, 196.
Return of Napoleon from St. Helena, Mrs. L. H. Sigourney, 219.

SABBATH MORNING (extract from The Sabbath), James Grahame, 132.
Sailor's Wife, The, Charles Mackay, 290.
Satan's Address to the Sun (extract from Paradise Lost), John Milton, 109.
Shepherd, The, to his Love, Christopher Marlowe, 224.
Shepherd's Life, The, Phineas Fletcher, 238.
Shepherd's Resolution, The, George Wither, 270.

Ship-builders, The, John G. Whittier, 205.
Silent Lover, The, Sir Walter Raleigh, 154.
Skylark, The, James Hogg, 178.
Snowdrop, The, Mary Robinson, 179.
Snowdrop, To the, Charlotte Smith, 180.
Song for a Highland Drover, Robert Bloomfield, 91.
Spirit of Spring, George Washington Doane, 208.
Spring, Description of, H. Howard, Earl of Surrey, 216.
Spring, The, Thomas Carew, 217.
Summer's Day, A (extract from the Seasons), James Thomson, 116.
Summer's Eve, Michael Drayton, 174.

Tears of Scotland, Tobias Smollett, 112.
Thames, The (extract from Cooper's Hill), John Denham, 138.
Three Fishers, The, Rev. Charles Kingsley, 20.
Tom Bowling, Charles Dibdin, 167.
Truth, Ode to (extract from Elfrida), William Mason, 236.

Universal Prayer, The, Alexander Pope, 142.

Vanity of Human Wishes (extract from), Samuel Johnson, 152.
Voice of the Morning, Charles Swain, 61.

Warden of the Cinque Ports, The, Henry Wadsworth Longfellow, 35.
Waterloo, Night before (extract from Childe Harold's Pilgrimage), Lord Byron, 27.
Wet Sheet and a Flowing Sea, Allan Cunningham, 213.
Widowed Mother, The, Professor Wilson, 236.
Wife's Funeral, The (extract from the Parish Register), George Crabbe, 218.
Wife's Tragedy, The, Coventry Patmore, 38.
Wild Flowers, Robert Nicoll, 168.

Yarrow Visited, William Wordsworth, 101.
Youth and Philosopher, The, William Whitehead, 122.

www.ingramcontent.com/pod-product-compliance
Lightning Source LLC
Chambersburg PA
CBHW030730230426
43667CB00007B/656